Let No Wheels Turn

The Wrecking of the Flying Scotsman, 1926

Margaret Hutcherson

ISBN: 1 901237 34 6

Printed and Published by TUPS Books
38 Hutton Close, Crowther Industrial Estate.
Washington, Tyne and Wear, NE38 0AH
Tel: 0191 419 0446 Fax: 0191 419 2647
Email: tupsbooks@aol.com

Photographs on pages, 3, 27, 29, 36, 38, 43, 68 are from the Hulton Library
collection.

Cover design by Peter Chapman

Richard Brierley,
1877—1957

This book is dedicated to my Grandfather, Richard Brierley of Cramlington, Northumberland. During the General Strike he was a shopkeeper of a general store at High Pit, having previously been a miner at Wrightson Pit, West Cramlington, where his son Peter worked. He eventually moved to London bringing his two youngest sons William and Edward with him.

When I was a young girl Grandfather told me how he and the miners of his villageplayed a part in the derailing of the Flying Scotsman during the difficult days of the General Strike of May 1926. With tears in his eyes he unrolled a wad of yellowing newspaper cuttings of that time, reporting the event, saying that one day I should write this story to tell of the desperate actions hungry men will take to fight for their rights.

It has taken a while, but Grandpa, I have kept my promise. This book is for you with my love and respect.

Acknowledgements

My love and thanks go especially to my husband Derek for encouraging my socialist views! Also to all my children for giving me the incentive to complete this book when my own enthusiasm began to falter and research seemed so complex. Special thanks to Kate who willingly gave me her word processor and instructions how to use it! To Wendy who patiently proof-read the near-finished article and declared it a 'good read,' to Nicolas for his enthusiastic railway research and to Matthew who patiently helped me to present the finished item with the wonders of modern technology. Thanks also to my cousins in Newcastle. To Joan for producing Grandpa Brierley's battered suitcase with its references, documents and old photographs and to Susan for her tireless local research and door knocking. To Enid, for her gems of local information, and also remembering Aunt Esther who passed away in 2005 aged 101. Her warm welcome and remarkable memories are treasured.

Particular thanks go to my friend and publisher David Temple who edited my manuscript and added additional research.

Finally, through my research I found my cousin Gordon and his family, who didn't even know I existed. Thank you all for your friendship and for putting together yet another piece of the jigsaw. Bless you all.

Foreword

by Ian Lavery
Chairman of The National Union of Mineworkers
and General Secretary of NUM, Northumberland Area

On the 10th May 1926 the miners of West Cramlington driven by hunger and desperation made a valiant attempt to stop coal trains driven by scab labour. The result was the derailment of the Flying Scotsman and eight men lost their freedom.

Ian Lavery

The great lockout of 1926, when miners refused to accept savage reductions in their already miserly wages and an increase in their hours of labour, will never be forgotten. In 1926 miners found themselves not just fighting the mineowners but the state. A state which organised scab labour, special police, introduced anti-trade-union legislation, organised a biased media utilising the BBC and newspapers specifically focused against the strike. They deliberately misreported events and manipulated statistics. Police intimidated witnesses to secure arrests and the judiciary handed out outrageous sentences.

Similarities with the miners strike of 1984 are all too apparent. The blind hatred of the miners expressed by Winston Churchill in 1926 was only surpassed by Margaret Thatcher in 1984 when she called the British miners 'the enemy within.'

Muckle, Sanderson, Baker, Harbottle, Stephenson, Ellison, Wilson, and Roberts are all true hero's of our labour and trade union movement. The actions of these honest, sincere hard working men will remain in our hearts forever and we will never forgive those who turned against them.

We owe our thanks to Margaret Hutcherson who has etched their names in history by producing this well researched and well written book.

Contents

Chapter 1   The Journey Begins   1

Chapter 2   Police and Propaganda   27

Chapter 3   Trial and Retribution   49

Chapter 4   No Regrets   85

Afterword   90

Sources   91

Chapter 1

The Journey Begins

The Merry Hampton

At 10 am on the morning of 10 May 1926, the seventh day of the General Strike, the Flying Scotsman was due to depart from Edinburgh Railway Station en route to London Kings Cross. On board were three medical students, Snowdon Blaiklock, Hope Pool and Duncan Livingstone, all from Edinburgh University. These young students were no ordinary passengers but were there to assist the train's guards.

The driver R Sheddon was a regular driver employed at Haymarket Depot Edinburgh and had 36 years service to his credit. On the footplate with him were two volunteer firemen Hird and Aitken, the latter having over six years engineering experience. Supervising the three students were two regular passenger guards Brown and Fletcher with 83 years experience between them. The volunteer ticket collector Murray had been on a brief signalmen's course after offering his services to the Railway company.

The Flying Scotsman was to be hauled by the locomotive Merry Hampton, a Pacific type engine No.2565 with an eight-wheeled tender. The train included 12 corridor coaches of the London and North Eastern

Railway (LNER) including a first class and a second class restaurant car. In the goods van was a cargo of perishables including churns of fresh milk and numerous creels of crabs and lobsters destined for the restaurants of London. These were classed as urgent and given priority of passage on all trains that could beat the strike.

The train departed from Edinburgh nine minutes late and the crew proceeded with some trepidation, and with good reason. There had been reports on previous days of hostility from strikers against both goods and passenger trains. Fletcher, one of the passenger guards, reported that on the previous day, he had stopped to open the crossing gates at Dam Dykes near Cramlington in Northumberland when a crowd of angry youths had shouted abuse and thrown stones at the train, breaking 20 windows. On the same day all the windows of the engine cab of another train had been smashed by stone-throwers on the down journey between Berwick and Newcastle.

The Flying Scotsman left Edinburgh and pulled into Berwick on Tweed without incident. Here Thomas Wedderburn, a permanent driver, stationed at Tweedmouth locomotive Depot, joined the train. He had 39 years service with the LNER, 27 of these as a driver. With Wedderburn safely aboard and well aware of the dangers that might lie ahead the crew eased the train out of Berwick Station to continue its journey to London. The next scheduled stop was to be Newcastle-upon-Tyne.

In the first class restaurant Duncan Livingstone was making flirtatious conversation with an attractive American passenger, forgetting for a while his duties as volunteer guard. His fellow students were going about their business as much as their brief training allowed. The remaining passengers settled into relaxing and reading, some closing their eyes to doze. The guards noted that many of the passengers had not chosen the usually popular window seats; no doubt the events of the previous days were weighing heavily on their minds. In the goods van the lobsters and crabs were surviving in their cramped containers unaware of their intended culinary destination.

The Flying Scotsman was now moving into hostile territory, the Great Northern Coalfield. This was the largest coalfield in Britain, extending from the north of Northumberland to the south of County Durham — 100 miles of pit villages populated by over 200,000 miners and their families. Communities that had endured decades of hardship and strife.

The General strike of 1926 was but the latest battle of an ongoing war between the Miners' Federation of Great Britain (MFGB) and the mineowners.

The MFGB had only achieved the status of a National Union in 1907 when the Durham Miners agreed to join. The first truly nationwide strike of miners began in 1912 when the miners struck work to achieve a national minimum wage. As in many disputes between men and management in the coal industry the strike was settled in Parliament by an act granting the miners a minimum wage to be negotiated on an area

Black labour opening crossing gates at Wooden Gate on Berwick to Newcastle line

basis. Most miners saw this only as a partial victory. A minimum wage agreed on an area basis, they argued, would tend to keep miners divided.

Eager to improve their industrial strength, in 1914, the MFGB combined with the National Union of Railwaymen and the National Transport Union in an organisation called the Triple Alliance. This alliance was forged on the principle that in the event that any of the three unions was attacked all would act in unison.

The declaration of war in 1914 brought no peace between miner and mineowner as the owners sought to take advantage of the crisis to claw back what few gains the miners had won. The owners' intransigence only added to the chaotic state of the industry, and eventually the Government was forced to take the pits into its control, a measure which guaranteed a level of profit to the owners.

In 1917 the success of the Russian Revolution had a profound effect on the thinking of both sides of the industrial divide. The Government and employers now looked upon any form of wide scale industrial unrest as revolutionary activity. For many working class leaders the revolution created a vision of what could be achieved.

When the First World War ended, the initial euphoria soon dissolved as it became apparent that the promise of a 'land fit for heroes' was not to be fulfilled without a fight.

On the January 13, 1919 the Miners' Union demanded a 30% increase in wages, a seven hour shift and the nationalisation of the mines under the control of the miners. Further demands were placed on the government by the other two unions of the Triple Alliance.

The nervousness of the government was demonstrated when on January 27, 1919 the shipyard and engineering workers on the Clyde struck work demanding a 40-hour week. The Government was swift to respond, moving tanks into Glasgow and arresting the strike leaders.

The tactics towards the miners was a little more subtle. They tried to

Miners dividing their pay 1920s

placate the union by setting up a commission under the chairmanship of Lord Sankey. The miners' union responded and withdrew the strike notice to allow the commission to sit. The interim report of the commission awarded a two–shillings per shift increase in wages and a reduction of the working day from eight to seven hours; and recommended the nationalisation of the coal industry.

Miners welcomed the report but it soon became evident that the Government had been playing for time when the Coal Commissioner refused to sanction any wage increases over 10% of the basic wage. When strikes against this order spread through the Yorkshire coalfield the Government deployed troops to suppress the strikes but had finally to climb down and withdraw the order.

In 1920 and again in 1921, when control of the mines was returned to the owners, the MFGB took strike action, testing the solidarity of the Triple Alliance which in both cases was found to be lacking. The failure of the alliance to come to the aid of the miners was the source of much bitterness in mining communities and earned it the nickname 'The Crippled Alliance.'

The early twenties were plagued by a general trade depression which suppressed the wages of all British workers, and by June 30, 1925 the coal owners were demanding further reduction in miners' wages, the abandonment of the minimum wage, the end to all national agreements and a return to local bargaining. The coalowners threatened to lock the miners out if they did not agree to these demands, demands which would reduce miners' conditions to those of 1900.

The General Council of the TUC now threatened supportive action in the event of a lockout. Tory Prime Minister Baldwin was not prepared for a showdown on this scale and to buy some time Parliament introduced a subsidy to the coal industry to avoid the reductions, and set up a second commission under the chairmanship of Lord Samuel.

While the commission was sitting Winston Churchill, who was directed by the Government to prepare for a war with the unions, constructed a strike breaking organisation called the Organisation For The Maintenance of Supplies (OMS). The purpose of this organisation was to recruit volunteers to replace striking workers in the event of a conflict. He also prepared for a propaganda war and planned the publication of a national newspaper to be call the *British Gazette*.

On March 10, 1926 the Samuel Commission reported its conclusion that a reduction in wages and an increase in hours was inevitable. Miners refused to accept the terms of the owners and on May 1, 1926 were locked out. The TUC tried to reach a compromise and when this failed invited their constituent bodies to strike in support of the miners on May 3, 1926.

Typical of the mining villages of the Great Northern Coalfield was that of West Cramlington, whose miners woke on that, Monday morning the May 10, 1926 to another day without work. This was alien to them, as working the pit at West Cramlington Colliery had been their way of life. At the age of fourteen all had left school to take their places at the colliery alongside their brothers, fathers, grandfathers and older school friends.

West Cramlington colliery opened in 1838. It employed 140 miners and at that time was considered to be the best-ventilated pit in Northumberland. The village was compact and of rectangular shape consisting of a row of terraced miners cottages in Lane Row. Across the southern end was Cross Road. Northward was Blue Bell Road, which continued into Freeholds.

Bait time at pit head Cramlington prior to general strike

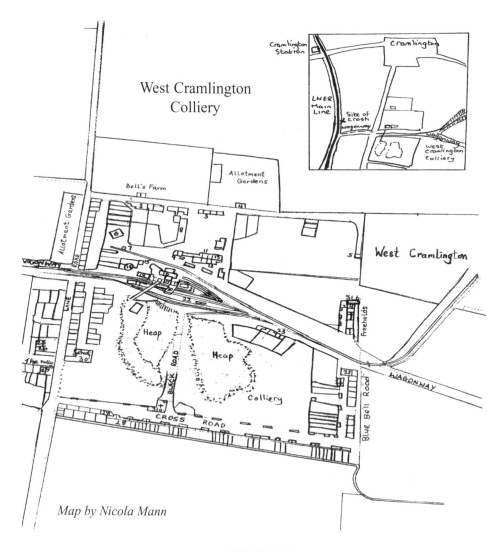

West Cramlington Colliery

Map by Nicola Mann

KEY TO MAP

1.	Bells Farmhouse	12.	Small Shop	23.	Railway Cottage
2.	Farm Workers Cottages	13.	Mechanics Institute	24.	Shop / Off-Licence
3.	Bells Cottages	14.	Pit Pond	25.	Stables
4.	Main Powder Magazine	15.	Pond Cottage	26.	Brewhouse
5.	Smaller Magazine	16.	Engine House (for No. 1) Pit	27.	Shop
6.	Engine House (for No.2 Pit)	17.	Pick Sharpeners Shop	28.	Master Shifters House
7.	No.2 Pit	18.	Pony Shaft	29.	Under Managers House
8.	Cattle Sheds	19.	No.1 Pit (Wrightson)	30.	School
9.	Blacksmiths	20.	Engine House	31.	(a)Prim. Meth. Chapel,
10.	Joiners Shop	21.	Screening Plant		(b)U.M. Chapel
11.	The Barracks	22.	Grease House	32.	Blue Bell Inn

Miners at Wrightson pit, Cramlington early 1920s

Within this rectangle were dwellings called the Barracks and Railway Cottages. Between the two coal heaps lay Black Road, so named for obvious reasons. Wrightson Pit was located in the northwest side of the village

A mineral line originally ran from the pit westward to join the London — Edinburgh mainline at West Cramlington Junction. This wagon way continued eastward past the Bay Horse Inn on to Seghill and eventually to the River Tyne. Another wagonway led to High Pit.

Almost all the houses were owned by the coalowners and the miners tenure was only as secure as their jobs — no job no house.

In addition the community had two Methodist Chapels, a pub called the Bluebell Inn, a school, a Mechanics Institute and a few essential shops.

There were slightly grander houses for the more senior pit-workers and managers. The site included the various trade workshops essential to the running of the colliery.

Since the start of the strike ten days earlier, efforts by the managers and the mineowners to keep the pits open had been thwarted by the striking miners. There were always pickets at the gates persuading potential blacklegs not to enter.

On the morning of the May 10 and about the same time as the Merry Hampton was pulling the Flying Scotsman out of Edinburgh station, a group of miners were making their way to a hastily organised meeting in the Miners Institute. Amongst them were four young men, Bob Harbottle, Bill Muckle, Tommy Roberts and Ollie Sanderson, all in their mid-twenties, all living in Lane Road, a stonethrow from the colliery entrance.

They would notice their local policeman Sergeant Graham standing near the steps keeping a watchful eye on 'his lads.'

The sergeant knew that there were a few that could cause 'devilment'

Tanks on the streets of London during the general strike

William Golightly

but he was not expecting trouble that day. The hall was packed tightly and a buzz of anticipation erupted as William Golightly, a member of the Northumberland Miners Association Executive Committee, arrived to address the meeting.

Golightly was an accomplished orator and ardent supporter of Arthur J. Cook, the leader of the MFGB. Golightly praised the miners for their loyalty to the strike and for their continued attempts to stop coal from being mined and transported. However, he observed, despite such efforts, still too much coal was reaching the furnaces of industry. He implored the miners, young and old, to redouble their efforts against the Government and to stop these trains.

'If you can't stop them at the stations, stop them between the stations,' he insisted. The meeting was noisy and at times a wave of hysteria gripped the assembly.

Golightly finished his speech, with his leader's famous words, 'let no wheels turn.' The cheers were deafening and the applause prolonged as the local miners' leaders pledged their support to the cause.

The miners of West Cramlington were now fired up and eager to follow Golightly's instructions. No real plans had been formed or decisions made, just a strong desire to get on with it. They had all been angered by Churchill's threat to send in the troops against the strikers. Already word had reached them of soldiers and tanks rumbling through the streets of London. There was some hope that as most of the troops were from working-class backgrounds there would be some who had divided loyalties.

The older men suggested to the youngsters that they should all go home for a bite to eat before taking any serious actions. And so hungry lads went home to meagre tables and agreed to meet later to discuss further tactics.

That afternoon the miners met at the trackside by the old wagonway, Golightly's words still uppermost in their thoughts — 'Stop them between the stations.'

At about this time, Martin, an engineer's assistant, was patrolling the mainline railway. His patrol was about seven miles away, between Barton Quarry and Plessey, four miles north of Newcastle. He left the Quarry with six volunteer platelayers. These blacklegs were mainly middle-class pro-government supporters or students, probably with little sense of politics but a desire for financial gain.

As they patrolled, they inspected the track and the rails, for damage or sabotage. When they arrived at Dudley council houses near Annitsford Station they were met by an angry mob of men and women, shouting abuse and using extreme foul language. Clods of earth, stones and ballast were hurled at the trackmen who first made a hasty retreat, then continued past Dudley level crossing, checking the chocks on their way.

At about 12.50 pm they reached Dam Dykes crossing, which was being patrolled by an ex-LNER police constable, with three assistants. The trackmen told them of their confrontation at Dudley before they continued toward Cramlington. They arrived at the old signal box, now being used as a platelayers' hut, where they found a cabin window had been removed but observed that all the tools and equipment appeared to be in place.

Martin noted that all the chocks were in position and the line appeared in good order. The trackmen now became aware of shouting and saw in the distance men running towards them from the east screaming abuse and gesticulating fiercely. Some were carrying tools and sticks. Groups of strikers then emerged from both sides of the railway, climbing over the fencing alongside the track. Others were congregating on a nearby bridge. A large group now approached from the wagonway which led from the mines to the main line. Miners of all ages were now shouting to the point of frenzy, desperate to vent their anger on these blacklegs.

'Scabs,' they shouted as they chased the now frightened trackmen towards the station at Cramlington. They picked up stones and ballast which they hurled at the trackmen.

'Kill the blacklegs', they threatened, 'Get their gear.'

Martin and his men were now proceeding at speed towards the station with 20 or 30 miners in pursuit. The stone-throwing continued and the men were struck repeatedly from behind, Martin sustaining a direct hit to his calf and another behind his ear.

For a while the chase continued but to the relief of Martin the mob eventually retreated — his tormentors had more important things on their minds.

The striking miners returned to the platelayers hut, where they hastily knocked down the locked door. Once inside the hut they selected the tools needed to lift out a rail. Possibly 30 miners in a state of released adrenaline and highly excited selected a rail on the down side track. Using sledgehammers they systematically knocked out the wooden chocks that held the rail in place. Bolts were loosened and fishplates removed. The rail was then rocked to loosen it from its fixing chairs on

13

the sleepers. Then with one final heave from many hands the rail was discarded alongside the track.

The now redundant chocks and tools were thrown to men outside the fence who in turn lobbed them into a pond not far from the wagonway. The adrenaline rush was now over. The deed was done. Surely this would stop the next train between the stations as Golightly had instructed. Coal-carrying trains would certainly be delayed this day and the blackleg labour that helped such trains run would be thwarted.

Some of the strikers at this point dispersed back to their homes not wishing to witness the consequence of their actions, but before the others had time to do more damage the miners heard in the distance the familiar sound of an approaching train. Muckle and his mates leapt the fence and hid in the bushes near the track while another group hid behind the platelayers cabin. One man ran northwards to warn the stationmaster.

Martin and his trackmen, their plusfours now dirty and mud-splattered had passed the unmanned signal box at the end of the platform and warned the stationmaster of the angry mob down the line, leaving him to warn oncoming trains.

Martin and his volunteers then resumed their patrol duties to the north of the station. It was now 1.50 pm and in the distance they too saw the steam of the approaching train.

Martin stood alongside the track waving his arms until the train eventually came to a stop 300 yards North of Cramlington station. He was surprised to see the train was not a coal train but the Flying Scotsman with passengers aboard. Martin warned the driver to expect a hostile crowd to the south of the station. He then decided to board the train with the rest of his patrol. Stopping only for a few words with the stationmaster at Cramlington station, Martin and his volunteers dispersed along the length of the train, warning staff and passengers to pull down the blinds and to keep away from the windows.

There was a buzz of excitement and fear as the passengers hastily organised themselves, while the medical students gave advice and reassurance to the passengers.

As the train proceeded towards the bridge, Aitken, the volunteer fireman, who was on the left of the footplate, noticed men standing on the bridge but failed to notice a warning from a young lad waving a red handkerchief.

The men on the footplate had been warned many times of the danger of missiles thrown from bridges, so instinctively they dived for the cover of the engine's cab.

In the train one woman, Mrs Farquarson, had, against all advice, been peeping from under the drawn blinds of the carriage when she saw men running from the trackside. Now in their hiding places these men were in for a terrible shock as they realised that the approaching engine was not pulling coal wagons but passenger carriages. They held their breath in awful anticipation willing the train to stop, but it continued on. When it reached the place where the rail was missing it first started to wobble to the left and right and then with a horrendous crash it slewed into the ballast, its momentum forcing it along the track.

 Passengers' screams were drowned by the screeching of metal on metal, the crunch of the engine ploughing into ballast, and the hissing of escaping steam as the driver applied his brakes. With the train still swaying left and right, gravity soon took over and still in forward motion, the engine 'keeled like a babe', toppling to the left. It became embedded in the embankment and finally came to rest by the platelayers' hut where the tools had been stolen. Still the screeching continued as the passenger carriages derailed, their momentum concertinaing the coaches onto either side of the track.

The miners hidden behind the platelayers' hut had a narrow escape. They were in shock and took flight. Muckle, from behind his bush, stayed petrified, frozen to the spot. When he turned to speak to his companions he realised that he was alone. They had fled in terror and so did he, as fast as his young legs would carry him, leaving behind a scene of complete devastation.

Billy Baker, a labourer, had been picking dandelions for his beloved canaries — a daily event. He was aware of what was happening but had not wanted to get involved. When the train crashed, he ran for his life with the others.

The Merry Hampton was on its side, steam hissing from its boilers. The tender and engine came to rest at an angle of 45 degrees. The first coach, still coupled, had concertinaed sideways across both tracks. The following coach had its bogeys ripped off and they lay scattered on the track. The coach itself landed astride the railway fence, its rear end lifting skywards. The third coach was pushed upwards and diagonally across the lines with its leading end wedged under the rear of the preceding coach. The fourth and fifth were also derailed and lay awkwardly across the track. The seven remaining coaches stayed on the rails.

Rails were bent at grotesque angles, bogeys lay scattered. Broken glass and twisted metal littered the scene.

When the engine came to rest, Wedderburn, the regular driver, shut off the steam and climbed out of the cab to dampen the fire from the engine with shovels of earth. He attended briefly to Aitken, who had a slightly scalded foot, and together the rest of the crew from the footplate made their way to the second carriage where they were able to assist passengers to safety.

Traumatised passengers began to emerge from the stricken coaches. They had first realised something was wrong when the coaches began to sway, then luggage fell from overhead racks, windows shattered as blinds were ripped from their fixings. At the point of impact passengers where thrown about like dolls, they held on to whatever they could and tried to protect their loved ones.

In the derailed carriages passengers were catapulted down the gangway landing abruptly at the fore end. In the immediate aftermath an eerie silence prevailed for a while as the enormity of the disaster became apparent. Then all hell was let loose. Hysterical passengers screamed as they realised that they were victims of a real train crash. Young children, unhurt but in shock, were separated from their parents and were now screaming for them. Many passengers had minor injuries, cuts and bruises and were in severe shock. Miraculously no one was killed.

Arthur Hamilton, a Government veterinary officer, lay trapped. His leg had been thrust through a window and was held fast under the ballast of the track. He was eventually released and placed in the care of the medical students.

In the goods van, amidst all the mayhem was the unreal sight of newly released live lobsters and crabs swimming around in the milk from the upturned churns, their journey now at an end.

Some of the 'wreckers' were seen regrouping by the trackside laughing and jeering. Others were reported running in all directions.

Martin the engineer, Brown the guard and a few servicemen on board who were uninjured, jumped down from the train and gave chase, but were deterred by the hostility of the villagers. There were to be no arrests that day. Brown retreated to the train, where noise and chaos still reigned.

The sound of the crash had been heard miles away and many hastened to the scene to help. Sergeant Graham, the local policeman, had been chatting to a farmer about a mile away. On hearing the dreadful screeching and subsequent crash he hurriedly cycled toward the scene. He met others running along the road from the direction of the colliery at West Cramlington. Wives and mothers gathered up towels and sheets expecting the worst. On their arrival hysterical women from the train rejected their help, calling them dirty miners' wives.

'Go home and wash your dirty selves and your dirty homes, we don't want help from the likes of you,' screamed one survivor.

In time the services arrived — police, fire engines, ambulances, railway officials and some servicemen. Dr. Quinn the local doctor hurried to the scene as did Dr. Dickie from Morpeth, Dr Allison from Newcastle, Dr Anderson from Seaton Delaval, along with members of the Cramlington Ambulance Brigade. Doctors Blackburn and Stabler were sent directly from the Newcastle Infirmary. When they saw the wreckage of the train they were all amazed that there were so few injuries and indeed no fatalities.

Those uninjured were ferried by buses to Newcastle, from where they would be able to continue their journey.

So many well-meaning people had given one injured man shots of spirits that by the time he reached the Infirmary at Newcastle he was reported to be quite merry and oblivious to his pain.

Sergeant Graham did his best to take statements at the scene, aware that some of his local lads may have been involved. He had himself been present at the union meeting that morning. Crowds of sightseers assembled at the railway fence but the Sergeant and others kept them off the track. Some of the young men were reported to have laughed and jeered. Sergeant Graham took a mental note of their names but for the moment made no comment or arrests. The men responsible had long departed the scene and returned to their homes.

Bob Harbottles' father met him in the lane near his home and just said 'you've done it now lad.'

There had been 30-40 men involved in the event on the line that afternoon and for the time being they all decided to keep their heads down and hope that no one noticed them.

At the scene of the crash the sightseers had been dispersed and the debris left for the expected investigation. A police patrol stayed behind to protect the scene until at about 5 pm, when Pemberthy the Permanent Way Inspector of Manors district arrived with a group of loyal staff to assist him. He had 18 years service in this post.

At the actual point of derailment he found a fishplate and a broken bolt lying at the end of a sleeper. Then clearing the ballast off the rail which was lying alongside of the track, he found it straight, undamaged and unmarked. He concluded that the rail had been deliberately taken out of the chairs prior to the accident.

He also noted that fishplates at both end of the rail had been removed. The men responsible must have had, he concluded, the proper tools and sufficient numbers of men in order to remove the rail from the chairs.

Under some bushes outside the railway fence, the platelayers found a quarter-pound hammer, a screw key, a pinch bar, and one fishplate, which paired with the one that had been found adjoining the sleeper. They also counted 24 wooden chocks, which had been removed from the pond. They made sketches and took notes of the damage to the track and the plate-layers cabin and noted the position of the engine, tender and coaches.

The work of clearing the line at Cramlington began immediately as both the north and south lines were blocked. Officials from the rail

View of missing fishplate

Work begins on clearing the line

company joined Pemberthy and his volunteers. Since most rail workers were on strike supporting the miners, they had to rely on what voluntary labour they could muster and were faced with what seemed at that time a formidable task. They first concentrated on doing only enough to clear and make safe the main line to the north. Under the guidance of Inspector Pemberthy about 40 willing volunteers worked throughout the night. Despite their aching limbs, blistered hands and lack of sleep they succeeded by 8 am to open the single track to the north. No doubt there were those in the village who had watched the night's events with a certain sense of guilt.

The wreckage on the line to the South was left as it lay awaiting the arrival of the official investigator for the Ministry of Transport, Colonel Pringle, who arrived on the morning of the May 12. Pringle examined the site and the position of the derailed carriages and engine and took note of how the site had been disturbed in order to open the northbound line. After hearing the evidence of eye-witnesses Pringle presented his findings to the Ministry of Transport at Whitehall on the May 27. He concluded that:

a) The railway company had taken such measures as were possible by

Line to north now clear — London Illustrated News

patrolling the line to ensure that the permanent way was in order for the passage of trains.

b) That the train in question was travelling at moderate speed when it was derailed and that the circumstances were such that no responsibility attaches to any of the engine men or railway personnel for the derailment.

c) That the derailment was due to the action by persons unknown, who maliciously removed a left hand rail from the down track and were engaged in further interference on both the up and down tracks when the train approached the scene of the accident. It appears therefore that a number of persons must have been engaged in this case of sabotage.

On the day that Pringle submitted his report to the Ministry the miners' union suffered a devastating blow when a majority of leaders of the TUC caved in and called off the General Strike.

At midnight on May 12th the General Strike ended. 'Victory for common sense,' was the universal verdict of the Press. The negotiating committee of the Tory cabinet under Stanley Baldwin had not ceased in their endeavours to win over the more moderate leaders on the TUC's General

Council and after ten days these leaders were faced with the choice of a constitutional crisis or an ignominious surrender. They chose surrender.

Now the miners leaders' were put under intense pressure from the Labour Party and TUC leaders to return to work under the owners' terms. Cook was urged not to make a 'tragic blunder' by Ramsay MacDonald, who asked if he could address the miners' executive himself. Cook declined the offer and the committee decided to continue the strike. They thanked all the industrial workers who had supported them over the ten days of the General Strike but bitterly condemned the TUC leaders who had deserted them.

The effectiveness of the strike was disputed and, as always in these disputes, the government were at pains to exaggerate the numbers at work and the efficiency of the black labour, while the miners insisted that the strike had been called off when it was getting stronger.

One indication of the effectiveness of the strike was demonstrated on May 13, when a message to the striking railwaymen from the LNER told the railwaymen that when the strike was over the number of staff the company could employ would be greatly reduced as the country's trade was substantially diminished and the tonnage of traffic to be handled would take time to recover.

The company wished it understood that preference would be given to those staff that offered themselves for employment without delay.

It was said that 12 striking miners offered their services for employment, fearing for their own jobs. Their offer was not accepted!

Slowly the wheels of industry began to turn and the country returned to near normality. There was no normality, however for the village of Cramlington, which now became the scene of an intensive police investigation. Crucial to this investigation was Sergeant Graham, who had been summoned to various enquiries in the immediate aftermath of the derailment. He was the man with the local knowledge. He had been near to the scene of the derailment and it was thought by his superiors that he must have witnessed the movements of the villagers as they fled to the safety of their homes.

It is fair to assume that Graham was in a dilemma. It was a difficult issue to cope with, as he had known the lads for many years. He knew their fathers and mothers and indeed had on many occasions had to issue fatherly warnings to some of the young offenders. A friendly chat with the father and a cup of tea with their mam was all that had been necessary. He may well have understood their desperation and the condition of near poverty in which they lived.

His reports at this time were non-commital and by the end of May no arrests had been made. But pressure was now being brought to bear on Graham to come up with some names.

On June 2 a question was raised in the House of Commons asking why the 'Cramlington Train Wreckers' had not been arrested and if there might be some encouragement to obtain evidence if a reward were to be offered. The Home Secretary, Sir William Joynson Hicks, replied that it was not general policy in cases of this kind to offer rewards.

During the following weeks the police were everywhere, asking questions and getting statements. Many miners were cross-examined but village solidarity endured. They remained loyal to each other. The miners' families knew who had been involved but hoped that if they all stuck together and did not co-operate with the police they would keep their sons and husbands safe at home.

Some police went incognito in order to ask questions informally in the pubs and even in the disguise of salesmen selling goods to the womenfolk, but in a tightly-knit community such as Cramlington these undercover men must have stuck out like sore thumbs.

One striker, Lyle Sidney Waugh, was the younger brother of a police constable who was one of Sergeant Graham's colleagues. He was also the nephew of a police inspector. Sergeant Graham certainly knew Lyle was involved but had at first withheld this information and had made no official report.

As pressure mounted for the local police to make progress, a man called Reddicliffe was arrested and charged with withholding information, a move probably intended to intimidate men who failed to co-operate. This incident may have frightened Waugh or more likely family pressure was applied to make him co-operate. Whatever the course of events it later became clear that Waugh made statements that implicated his workmates and his neighbours in the derailment. As rumours circulated the solidarity of the village cracked and six other strikers were induced to turn king's evidence in the hope that they too would avoid prosecution.

For several days after Waugh's statement had divided the village there was a flurry of police activity among the terraced houses of Cramlington. Visits to and from the police station were made and mothers looked accusingly at each other.

On Saturday June 5 just before midnight the arrests began. One by one, under the cover of darkness, the police arrived and took miners from their homes.

Billy Baker, a young, quiet labourer, and Jimmy Ellison were arrested from their homes at Freeholds. Baker's wife was distraught as he was dragged from his home. She knew he had not been involved.

Bob Harbottle, Ollie Sanderson and Tommy Roberts from Lane Road were also taken. Roberts had not long returned to the mines having recently been demobbed from the Indian army, where he had fought on the North West Frontier. He had just enjoyed a good night out spending some of his well-deserved demob pay.

Bill Stephenson and his wife had retired to bed early before being awakened by a hammering on the door. Bill was unceremoniously despatched to the cells.

Tommy Roberts

Wallace and Wilson were next. For Arthur Wilson's wife Rose it was to be a double shock, as her younger brother was Bill Stephenson.

Bill Muckle was the last. He had left home earlier that evening to meet his girlfriend Dora at Cullercoats, a walk of about five miles. As he passed the pub in the village he met three lads and one said, 'Have a good night Bill, it may be the last one for a while.' Muckle had heard rumours that someone had 'spilled the beans' but continued on his way hoping that they were not right. On his return in the early hours of the morning he stopped for a chat with a few of his mates who hadn't yet gone home. They were at the end of the street sitting on a log when four policemen pounced on Bill and took him away immediately. He had no time to say goodbye to his mother, who was waiting at home knowing the police were out looking for her son, but powerless to warn him.

The next morning the whole village woke to learn of the night-time arrests.

Chapter 2

Police and Propaganda

Student volunteers at work during the general strike

The derailment of the Flying Scotsman at Cramlington was perhaps the most spectacular incident of the General Strike but it was not unique. Churchill's OMS had recruited an army of strike-breakers drawn almost exclusively from the middle classes, exposing a clear division in 1920s society. In particular the Government recruited ex-servicemen, students and undergraduates. Their training was minimal and consequently the risks were great. On the railways this lack of training caused many accidents and there were many near misses.

Medical students were excused lectures as long as they were engaged

TO ALL WORKERS IN ALL TRADES.

- Additional Guarantees.
-- Official,

Every man who does his duty by the country and remains at work or returns to work during the present crisis will be protected by the State from loss of trade union benefits, superannuation allowances, or pension. His Majesty's Government will take whatever steps are necessary in Parliament or otherwise for this purpose.

STANLEY BALDWIN.

in keeping the essential services running. Trams, buses, trains and commercial vehicles were manned by blackleg labour and such was the enthusiasm that far more volunteered than could be employed.

The railways were a popular choice for the volunteers, either as platform staff or passenger train guards, while others took almost schoolboy delight in being offered jobs on the engine as assistant fireman. One student from the Newcastle College of Medicine recalled,

We had a great sense of power as we sailed through the ticket barriers calling out 'platelayer.' A word to the driver and he stopped his train at our training depot. After several hours of backbreaking training at laying and removing rails, we made our way, very dirty, to the line, where we held up the next train, climbed aboard and travelled freely to Central Station. We had no sense of politics. It was great fun without parental supervision and the unskilled wage was gratefully received.

However many of his fellow volunteers were so blistered by the end of the first day they did not show up for work the following day.

For helping the government break the strike these blacklegs were universally hated within the mining communities and many acts of sabotage occurred throughout the country. Trains carrying coal were

Propaganda photograph showing well-heeled women 'volunteers' during General Strike

repeatedly stoned from both the track -side and the bridges. Signalmen were 'persuaded' by the picketing strikers to abandon their signal boxes and level crossing gates were repeatedly smashed.

The strike did on occasion bring lighter moments. A train being driven by a retired railwayman overshot the platform at Newcastle Central Station to the amusement of all those picketing. One striking Geordie couldn't resist the quip, 'Divven bother hinnie, you stay where you are — we'll just move the platform to you.'

The miners' hatred for the middle-class blacklegs paled into insignificance when compared with their feelings towards those members of their own class who broke the strike.

Men from the same mining villages who gave their labour to the mine-owners had to be escorted to their work by huge contingents of police and servicemen. Poverty and hunger drove men to carry out acts of revenge and blacklegs' homes were vandalised. Wives and families whose breadwinners were at work were abused by the whole village.

A popular form of ritual humiliation was a practice known as 'tinpanning'. The women of a village, armed with spoons and tin pans or pokers and blazers would follow a strike-breaker when he left home, banging on the tinpans and hurling abuse.

To restrain acts of sabotage and revenge the Government recruited thousands of extra police. These 'special constables' were organised in different sections with instructions to support the blackleg workers and to arrest offenders in strategic sensitive locations.

In Newcastle the hallowed turf of St. James' Park, Newcastle United's football ground, was used for recruitment and training of the 'specials'. In just a few days 1,500 men were recruited and organised into eight main sections. Men who were ex-forces were given immediate responsibility.

The mounted section recruited 44 men and 22 horses working around the clock in shifts.

Specials at St James' Park during general strike

The Light Car section had 350 men and over 150 cars. These were to be used for speedy access to trouble spots. There were 18 vehicles and 40 men for the Heavy Vehicle Section used for the rapid conveyance of police in large numbers. 80 men and 80 motorbikes formed patrols and were used to co-ordinate the activity of the various units by carrying important messages and documents.

60 men were allocated point duty and were to arrange the protection of Government convoys and to secure country routes. 12 special constables were given the administrative task of issuing passes, identity cards and clothing to the remaining foot section of over 900 recruits. All were held in reserve at the football ground where they received their basic training.

The *Newcastle Weekly Chronicle* was impressed and reported that during the crisis there had been many reasons for congratulating the City Police and members of the Special Constabulary associated with them:

One department in particular at the Central Police Station run by Sergeant George Strangeways deserved special praise. As the enrolment of the 'specials' began, he was suddenly faced with the necessity of increasing his staff numbers, particularly due to the records required. To this end he enrolled two gentlemen of proven organising abilities, Major C.H.Mortimer and Mr.E.Chalker. With these two gentlemen and a small but keen band of 'specials,' attention was given to the details of the improvised organisation of over 1,500 men passing through their hands without a hitch. The work of all these staff was purely voluntary, yet each one was eager to put in a full day's work, sometimes not finishing until after midnight.

The 'specials' were in action from the first days of the General Strike, when hundreds of strikers blockaded the High Level Bridge and the Quayside in Newcastle. Reports estimated that 700-800 strikers had rolled up their sleeves and were shouting, 'Into the police, into them!'

The police and specials countered with a baton charge resulting in many bloodied casualties. Under the Emergency Powers Act (EPA) the police could arrest and hold anyone who was found to be involved in anti-government activities such as intimidation and wilful damage.

On May 9, 31 miners were charged in Newcastle with acts 'calculated to prevent the proper use of the highway' when a crowd of more than 400 stopped all traffic and broke windows of buses belonging to the United Bus Company.

On another occasion ten miners were charged with an attempt to set fire to a newspaper van carrying copies of *The Times.*

Despite the best efforts of the constabulary, the acts of obstruction and sabotage continued. Cells through out the area were packed with strikers, Many more avoided capture, causing chaos and confusion on the roads and the railways

The Unions claimed the strike was almost 100% effective and denounced

London bus manned by strikebreakers — London illustrated News

the strikebreaking activity of the Government as ineffective and disastrous. The Government, however, was telling a different story. The pages of the *British Gazette* were filled with articles praising the work of the volunteers and exaggerating their effectiveness. On one occasion it reported that 3,000 trains had run on the previous day. Even if this figure was correct the *British Gazette* did not inform its readers that this figure represented under ten per cent of the normal daily traffic.

This propaganda battle was crucial and given high priority by both sides.

As soon as the General Strike had been announced, Winston Churchill initiated his plan to publish a daily edition of a newspaper to keep the mineowners' and government's loyal followers informed.

Churchill wasted no time in persuading the *Morning Post* to offer their premises and printing facilities. Churchill then appointed himself editor and named this newspaper *The British Gazette*. Each day the newspaper

TO-DAY'S CARTOON.

By BERNARD PARTRIDGE.

UNDER WHICH FLAG?

JOHN BULL : ONE OF THESE TWO FLAGS HAS GOT TO COME
DOWN—AND IT WON'T BE MINE.

General strike cartoon from British Gazette

34

featured a political cartoon usually depicting the unions as treacherous enemies of the state.

The first edition appeared on May 5 and the last issue on May 13. It consisted of a four-page large format spread with a circulation of over two million copies a day.

Its language, however, proved too strong for some in the government, and after only a few editions Prime Minister Baldwin had to appoint a senior minister to 'blue pencil' some of Churchill's more inflammatory remarks and comments.

Police were on constant patrol outside the offices of the Morning Post to prevent opponents blockading the distribution or sabotaging the paper's production. Churchill was totally uncompromising to the point, it is said, that he refused to report the results of a friendly football match between some Plymouth strikers and the local police because the strikers had won the match.

The General Council of the TUC was equally determined that its version of events would be heard, and produced its own official bulletin, *The British Worker*, in co-operation with the editors of the *Daily Herald*. The first editorial was at pains to make clear that the paper reflected 'the supreme authority' of the industrial section of the British Labour Movement — The Trades Union Congress. The General Council held a tight grip on the paper's content and everything published had to be approved by its Press and Publicity Committee. The paper's editor was to recall that, the first day was very exciting and busy and it was touch and go whether the publication would go ahead at all.'

The General Council decided that the *British Worker* would be an evening paper, and when news of the publication of the first edition reached the streets a large crowd gathered outside the offices of the *Daily Herald*. The cheering and applause soon bought the police in large numbers, and mounted police attempted to clear the crowds. A contingent of plain-clothes police ordered the proprietor to close down the press.

Strikers and police football teams at Plymouth Argyle football ground

They had been issued with a warrant giving them the power to search the premises and seize all copies of the last issue of the *Daily Herald,* which they said was subversive. Having gained access to the building on this pretext they then proceeded to confiscate copies of the first edition of the *British Worker* for submission to the City Commissioner.

When the General Council was informed of the raid they contacted the Labour Party, who remonstrated with the Government. The ban was lifted and again the presses started to roll and the first edition of the *British Worker* was launched shortly after midnight.

On May 11 the British Worker reported the derailment of the Flying Scotsman. It also reported that at about the same time at St. Margaret's in Edinburgh misjudgement by volunteer labour caused a passenger train from Berwick, also being manned by blacklegs, to crash, killing three people and injuring 16 others.

The first edition of the *British Worker* had consisted of eight pages but when the Government commandeered paper supplies the editor was forced to reduce the number of pages by half. The editor issued the following statement:

The Prime Minister, by attempting to stifle the voice of Labour, runs

THE
BRITISH WORKER
OFFICIAL STRIKE NEWS BULLETIN
Published by The General Council of the Trades Union Congress

| No. 7. | TUESDAY EVENING, MAY 11, 1926. | PRICE ONE PENNY |

ENGINEERS TO STOP TO-DAY

Shipyards Also : Orders Welcomed

STRIKE SPREADS

So far from " dribbling back," as Mr. Churchill pretends, the men on strike are standing like a rock, and more are coming out.

To-morrow another section of the Movement will be called into action, the order having gone forth that the engineering shops and shipyards are to stop to-night.

The order applies to all unions in the engineering and shipbuilding trades affiliated to the Trades Union Congress.

It does not apply to men engaged at the Government dockyards, Admiralty establishments, or Government engineering works.

The men have awaited the instructions impatiently, and all over the country they received their marching orders with enthusiasm and a sense of relief.

In addition to the men obeying this call to reinforce the gallant " first line," others are out, either because of

MORE UNIONS OUT

The Amalgamated Moulders, Shipyard workers, and members of the Amalgamated Engineering Unions as well as General Engineering Unions will not start work to-morrow.

refusal to work with blacklegs, or because the pressure of the strike is closing down the factories.

Some of the very small percentage of N.U.R. members who hesitated at first have now joined up.

Not a single area has weakened," is Mr. Cramp's report.

At Bradford 7,000 operative dyers ceased work yesterday because of the introduction of blackleg transport.

Twenty-five thousand operative dyers are now out in Lancashire and York-shire.

The general position in Preston is unchanged, the men remaining confident of winning the fight.

NO SLACKENING

Cabinet's New Tactics Defeated by Indisputable Facts

The Cabinet and its supporters have dropped Mr. Churchill's " Revolution " stunt.

The " Times " says to-day in a leading article : " No one suggests for a moment that any considerable number of men on strike are animated by revolutionary motives."

That marks the end of Mr. Churchill's foolish and dangerous gamble. Now the Cabinet's tactics are changed. Now the official gramophones are grinding out the statement that strikers are going back to work.

This is as much a fabrication as the other. The number of strikers has not diminished; it is increasing. There are more workers out to-day than there have been at any moment since the strike began.

They will stay out until they are instructed by Headquarters to return to work.

THE REAL TRUTH OF THE COAL NEGOTIATIONS

Chairman of General Council Replies to Sir Douglas Hogg

In the Government publication, the *British Gazette*, of this morning, appears an article by the Attorney-General, Sir Douglas Hogg, which purports to state the truth of the coal negotiations. As one who has been directly associated with those negotiations, I claim the right to speak with a degree of authority on this matter which neither the Attorney-General nor anyone else with second-hand information can possibly possess.

The initial cause of the deadlock was the mineowners' arbitrary attitude in refusing to conduct national negotiations as recommended in the Commission's Report, and their action in giving notices to enforce a general reduction in wages.

From the moment the mineowners issued lock-out notices to their workpeople, the question at issue, so far as the General Council was concerned, was the withdrawal of those notices as a condition preliminary to the conduct of negotiations. From that we have never receded.

The Government representatives insisted that the mineowners must first declare themselves definitely as willing to accept a reduction in wages.

In these circumstances, and in view of the inevitability that there would be a stoppage throughout the coalfields on May 1 if the notices and demands of the mineowners were pressed, the General Council decided to call a conference of the responsible Executives of the unions

CONTINUED ON PAGE FOUR

FIVE RAILWAY CRASHES

Sequel to Blackleg and " Voluntary " Labour

FOUR DEAD

The attempt to work the intricate mechanism of the British railway system by " volunteer " and blackleg labour has already had a tragic sequel.

No fewer than five serious passenger train accidents occurred yesterday and this morning—two of them resulting in loss of life.

The worst occurred yesterday afternoon on the L.N.E.R. at St. Margaret's, Edinburgh.

While a number of wagons were being shifted from the up to the down main line a passenger train from Berwick, manned by a blacklegs, crashed into them. Three people were killed, 16 injured.

About the same time the " express " train from Edinburgh to King's Cross jumped the line between Annisford and Cramlington. The engine and first coaches overturned and caught fire. No one was killed.

At Bishop's Stortford a goods train. The goods engine and two passenger coaches were derailed and the station partially wrecked. One body has been recovered from the wreckage.

This morning an electric train from Elmhurst, running into Victoria Station, failed to stop in time and collided with a stationary coach.

At Hull on Monday night a " volunteer " ran his engine into some stationary wagons. He himself was severely injured.

These accidents—all within the space of 24 hours—are a grim commentary on the claim of the companies and the Government that something like a " normal " train service is being restored.

" Accidental death " was the verdict returned to-day at the inquest on C. A. Moon, a young engineer's draughtsman, living at Guildford. He volunteered to act as a passenger guard on an electric railway, stepped on a live rail, and was instantly killed.

Published for the General Council of the Trades Union Congress by Victoria House Printing Company, Carmelite-street, London, E.C.A. Telephone (6 lines) : 8212 City.

PASS THIS ON OR POST IT UP

37

Unloading newsprint in London under police guard

the very grave risk of undoing all the good that has been done by the General Council's daily appeal to strikers to behave in an orderly manner. His action is provocative.

Publication and distribution of the newspaper was patchy and delayed by transportation problems and in all it ran just eleven issues, the last being on May 17.

The extreme reaction of the government to the publication of *The Worker* demonstrated just how important the government viewed this propaganda war. They wished to maintain anti-strike papers to persuade the public that the strike was ineffective. For the unions *The Worker* was the only means of communication available to keep their members informed and to encourage them to believe that their actions were both valuable and successful.

Such was the thirst for news that one centrally produced newspaper could not cope and small locally produced radical news sheets, produced on clandestine duplicators, sprang up all over the country. Often striking print workes from both national and local papers played a role in the production of these unofficial bulletins. Front pages often urged the reader to 'Paste it up or pass it on.'

In the North there were two such daily papers printed throughout the strike. The Blaydon and Chopwell District Council of Action printed *The Northern Light* at the cost of a penny. Its first issue appeared on May 5, in which the editor explained the conditions under which they were working:

> We have had to live in an atmosphere of possible police raids. We are always ready and prepared for that event with duplicate premises, editor and machines. Thus in such a raid we would still publish. There is a constant cat and mouse game as the police do their best to crush this publication.

Volunteers on motorbikes distributed the papers to the picket sites at the railway stations and in the mining villages. Sympathetic local traders lent vans and labour to assist publication and distribution throughout the North.

The Workers Chronicle was a double paged spread, published by the Newcastle Trades Council at the cost of a halfpenny. The Editor explained that the publication was to:

> Provide the working class with [assistance in] the great struggle into which we have entered in defence of wages and hours. We will also indicate the kind of policy necessary to give victory to the workers. Every instruction possible received from the General Council in London will be published in the next issue of the Workers Chronicle.

Early headlines read, 'Stand firm,' 'Be men, there will be casualties.' 'Cowards flinch in the face of foe', and a message to the women read, 'Stand by your men.'

Each issue included satirical cartoons, lampooning the Government, mineowners and heads of industry. The daily progress of the strike action was recorded — acts of sabotage and successful action against the local blacklegs. With so much hostility from the establishment these unofficial publications must have given the strikers a big moral boost.

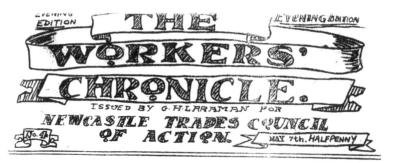

Extracts from The Workers Chronicle duplicated and circulated in Newcastle on Tyne in the days between May 6th and May 14th 1926.

STAND FIRM

Comrades and fellow workers,the Prime Minister has called upon the Nation to stand steady. On behalf of the Trades Council ,I also ask you to stand steady.The crisis which has arisen constitutes an attack upon the economic standards of the miners and all workers of this country. There has never been such a position as this in the whole industrial history of Britain. Never has there been a greater need for workers to stand solid.Our sympathy is and will be in favour of the miners. It is quite obvious that should we fail in this great struggle,we in other trades will undoubtedly be defeated.A United Front will defeat the efforts of the Capitalists and their Government to cut wages again. So again I say,be firm and thus secure victory. G.H.LARAMAN(PRESIDENT)-NEWCASTLE & GATESHEAD TRADES AND LABOUR COUNCIL
-----ooOoo-----
WELL DONE
ALL BUSES STOPPED AT CHESTER-LE-STREET. Every worker employed by the General Bus Co.is out on strike in support of the miners.Not a Bus is running and the pickets are very active.

" "

BOYCOTT THE
BOSS PRESS
" "

(This Page from the First Edition-May 6th 1926)

YOUR MASTER'S VOICE

IT'S YOUR WAGES I WANT

A MESSAGE TO THE WOMEN
I would urge all women to analyse and try to understand the position. Stand foursquare behind the menfolk, remembering that their fight is our fight and that of the children. All right thinking people are with us and I especially appeal to all mothers to watch the position of their girls.Help them to resist the temptation to blackleg on our men. JESSE T.PLATT.NAT.UNION OF GEN.& MUN. WORKERS.

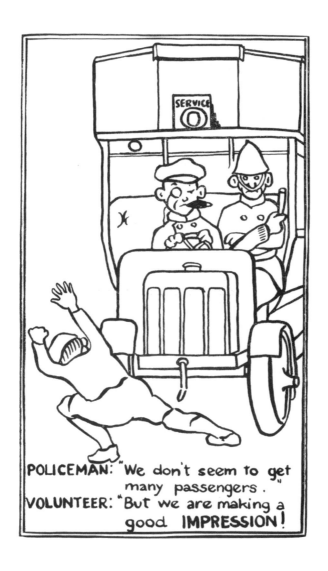

General strike cartoon from St. Pancras Bulletin May 10

General strike cartoon from St. Pancras Bulletin May 6

Prior to the strike the national and local newspapers published as normal and were universally hostile to the miners and the TUC. At midnight May 3 the printing unions withdrew their labour and national and local papers were only then produced erratically with black labour.

Almost every London newspaper produced some kind of edition with the help of volunteer labour. The newspaper proprietors' troubles, however, were not at an end once their papers were produced. There was still the problem of distribution.

The *Newcastle Echo and Chronicle* with the help of strike-breakers continued printing throughout the strike. However, picketing on the main routes, particularly in mining areas, made the loading and distribution a hazardous operation. Cars and vans from the newspaper depots were targeted and stopped. Drivers were berated and their papers stolen and burnt. Tyres were slashed and drivers pulled from their cabs, in some instances causing injury.

On one occasion pickets attacked a *Chronicle* van and ran off with a large number of newspapers, but the police caught up with the raiders outside Newcastle and forced them to reload the van.

Each day the police made arrests and the courts were inundated.

Despite all the efforts of both sides of the divide to suppress each other's publication, in the main these papers continued to be printed and distributed to some degree, however spasmodically.

The Government had access to a means of communication for which the TUC had no comparable equivalent — the wireless.

Catching up with the news

Prime Minister Stanley Baldwin

The British Broadcasting Company had been formed in 1922 and was a private organisation only gaining its first Royal Charter in 1927. John Reith, the managing director, had the high-minded belief that the BBC was, 'For the people, to entertain, inform and educate.'

It was Reith himself who announced to the listeners that the General Strike had begun.

Churchill felt that during the strike the BBC should be commandeered as a propaganda mouthpiece for the Government. Baldwin, a long-standing friend of Reith, sensed that it would be shrewder to allow Reith to continue to give 'impartial' news and views to the general public.

However, all BBC transmissions were censored by JCC Davidson, Baldwin's closest political confidant and parliamentary secretary to the Admiralty. Each day during the strike there were five news bulletins and a daily review they called an 'appreciation of the situation,' which gave both pro- and anti-strike information. After censorship these were transmitted from the BBC station at Savoy Hill London.

AJ Cook

Churchill was not happy with even this degree of impartiality. He resented the strikers' being given any positive feedback at all. He wanted such positive information 'muffled,' but Reith resisted vehemently.

Memories of Churchill's activities during the Great War were still in people's minds. He was still a controversial figure and not fully trusted by the general public. Baldwin and Davidson no doubt recognised this and continued to oppose the Government taking over the BBC. It would, they argued, only retain public confidence as long as it appeared to be impartial. The BBC therefore continued to quote from the speeches of the Trade Union leaders and articles from the *British Worker.*

Under this cloak of impartiality, misleading Government propaganda was broadcast. The numbers returning to work were exaggerated and although challenged by the unions the inflated figures were never corrected.

When the General Strike ended on May 12 it was Reith who informed the nation from his studio at his own home in Barton Street. This venue was arranged to protect Baldwin, who with Ramsay MacDonald also broadcast a statement, from the crowds at Savoy Hill. After Baldwin and MacDonald had given their respective addresses Reith read a message from King George V:

> Our country can be proud of itself, as during the last nine days there has not been a single shot fired and no one killed. It shows what wonderful people you are.

He then read from the radical hymn, Blake's Jerusalem, with a full orchestra and chorus joining in at the last verse. Such a rousing emotional broadcast reflected just how relieved the establishment was that the strike had been called off. Reith was knighted the following year.

The papers reacted to the end of the strike in similar vain: 'Victory for Common Sense,' wrote the *Daily Chronicle.*

The reaction of *The British Worker* was upbeat but must have puzzled many strikers, who condemned the action of the TUC as a betrayal of the miners.

The British Worker's conclusion was that:

There has never been in this or any other country such a marvellous demonstration of working class solidarity as the General Strike **which achieved its object today**. [our emphasis]

Arthur Pugh, chairman of the TUC (second left) leaving 10 Downing street after calling off the general strike

Not all trades returned immediately owing to restrictions placed upon them by the employers. Attempts to penalise them for striking was thwarted when the unions threatened further strike action.

The miners throughout Britain were left to struggle on alone.

Mounted police charge at Elephant and Castle, London during general strike

Chapter 3

Trial and Retribution

The Moot Hall, Newcastle

The miners arrested in Cramlington on the night of June 5 and the early hours of June 6 were each taken to the police station at Gosforth, a suburb to the north of Newcastle, where they were held in separate cells. Although none of them could have been surprised that they were in this predicament it must now have become clear just how serious a situation they were facing.

They were questioned throughout the night, none of them knowing who had been arrested or what they might have said or who had given evidence against them.

On Monday June 7, the next day, the nine men were taken to a police court at The Moot Hall, Newcastle before magistrates Ellis, Westmancott, and Irwin. The Miners' union could not have been informed of this development, as the men were entirely without legal representation.

The prosecution was led by TH Smirk, who charged the men with:

> Having at West Cramlington on May 10, feloniously, unlawfully and maliciously displaced a certain rail and other things belonging to and connected with the London and North Eastern Railway with intent thereby to overthrow an engine, tender and carriages using the said railway.

Now the accused were to find out who had turned king's evidence when Smirk called Lyle Sidney Waugh, the constable's brother, to the witness stand.

According to newspaper reports Waugh said that at about 1 am on Monday May 10 he had been standing on the corner end near the Blue Bell public house. He went along the colliery way to Lane Row railway crossing with Robert Taylor, George Wardle and William Reddicliffe, the miner charged on Saturday for withholding information. They stood for some minutes and then went towards the LNER railway.

A number of men were about eight yards away and they were tampering with the railway. There was a big bunch of them and they were stooping, trying to lift the rail. Amongst them were the accused, and Waugh recalled that he heard the sound of hammering.

After hearing Waugh's evidence the clerk of the court Mr WV Mulcaster asked the accused if they wanted to ask the witness any questions. They were cautioned not to incriminate themselves.

For the first time facing their accusers, threatened with imprisonment and without legal representation, the defendants threw caution to the wind and turned on Waugh.

Harbottle accused Waugh of being with them on the railway and said that Waugh himself had lifted the plate. Waugh immediately denied the accusation.

Wilson supported this accusation and added that he had heard Waugh shout, 'haad away lads lift the rail oot.' Two other miners repeated the same accusation, which Waugh continued to deny.

Wallace asked if Waugh had seen him on the line. Waugh responded that he was not sure.

The exchanges became more heated as the accused men started to quiz Waugh about other miners who had been present but whom Waugh had not named.

The *Newcastle Journal* reported the following exchange:

Wilson to Waugh: Why did you not give all the names?

Waugh: I gave the names of all I was nearly sure of.

Wilson to the bench: He knew everybody who was there because he was on the job himself.

Wilson: Did you go home and change your clothes?

Waugh: Yes I did.

Wilson: Who told you that the inspector knew some of the men by the clothes they wore?

Waugh: Everybody was saying that.

Wilson: I told you. Did you run away?

Waugh: Yes I didn't want to be in it at all.

This all must have been music to the prosecution's ears. Wilson's outburst was the most damaging when he said to the bench,

There is another 29 to come up who did the work the same as us.

The court heard evidence from Tommy Hills, who gave specific evidence against his friend Jimmy Ellison. This was a particular blow to Ellison, who had often accompanied Hills to Gosforth Park racecourse to help him sell ice cream.

Taylor, Wardle and Dodds all appeared as witnesses for the prosecution to condemn their former comrades, Wardle implicating all the accused except Wallace and Sanderson.

All the defendants were remanded in custody for seven days pending committal proceedings and all were refused bail. As the hearing ended, wives and mothers sobbed as they pressed forward to give their men packages of cigarettes and food.

In court that day was a press reporter called Richard Bell, who had been taking shorthand notes of the proceedings.

At a further remand hearing Wallace and Reddicliffe were released for lack of evidence and on June 26 the remaining eight prisoners were formally charged and committed to appear at the quarterly assizes on July 30 at the Moot Hall.

The charges against them now differed from those presented to the police court. In addition to the charge of removing a rail to overturn an engine were two more charges:

1. The intent to endanger the safety of certain persons and certain other things travelling or being upon the said railway.

2. Endangering the safety of passengers contrary to section 34 of the Offences Against the Person Act 1861.

In the same court that day there was a poignant reminder of 1920s hardship. A young mother was also committed to the assizes having been accused of murdering her own baby. She pleaded that she had been unable to provide for its needs and could not bear to see it starve.

Now things were looking decidedly black for the Cramlington men. The introduction of the further charges of intent to endanger life made the consequences of a guilty verdict far more serious.

Any thoughts of a sympathetic jury were tempered with the knowledge that in 1926 jurors were not selected from the general population. To be a juror you had to be a ratepayer and to pay rates you had to own property.

Miners living in their tied cottages did not own property and there was little sympathy for miners among property holders of Newcastle.

On July 30 the trial began of Stephenson, Harbottle, Sanderson, Muckle, Baker, Ellison, Wilson and Roberts before the Honourable Sir Robert Alderson Wright.

The relatives of the accused and many of their friends and workmates packed the benches of the public gallery. Outside the court many more miners and their family crowded the square.

They had been warned that this case would probably go on into a second day. Muckle's mother stood staunch and straight-faced as the evidence was read. She was a large imposing woman wearing her Sunday best, her son's girlfriend Dora Murphy by her side. Mrs Ellison and Mrs. Wilson were both in court with their children. Journalists from both local and national newspapers packed the press benches.

The Northumberland Miners' Association provided Archibald Wilson and CB Fenwick to represent the miners while CF Lowenthal led the prosecution.

Opening for the Crown CF Lowenthal told the court,

> There is ample evidence to prove the guilt of the accused. I don't say that they were the only ones concerned in this business. It may be there are others. It is quite immaterial if hereafter it is possible for the crown to show that other men not yet brought before the court were parties to the crime. They will be brought before one of His Majesty's courts and dealt with according to their deserts.

He then concentrated on the further charges included in the June 26 hearing, arguing that it was inconceivable that in removing the rail the accused had not intended to do harm to the passengers on the train.

The first witnesses called by the prosecution dealt with the events leading up to the derailment, none of which were in dispute.

Lyle Sidney Waugh was the first miner called to give specific evidence against the eight accused miners.

The Morpeth Herald and Reporter on August 2 gave the following report:

Lyle Sidney Waugh, miner, repeated previous evidence. He told of going with George Wardle, William Reddicliffe and Robert Taylor to the railway where he had seen the men who had hold of the rail. He knew all eight men, mostly for all of his life and identified them as the accused. He with others went near the scene of the displaced rail. When they saw steam of the engine in the distance they left and when they heard [the crash] they ran away.

Cross-examined by Mr Wilson the witness denied that he was the ring-leader of the party who had removed the rail.

Mr Wilson: When did you make up your mind to give your friends away.

Mr Lowenthal objected to the question as being unfair and could be asked in two parts.

Mr Wilson: Are you friends with the accused men.

Waugh: I am.

Mr Wilson: Why did you give the names to the police?

Waugh: To save another man from getting time (he was referring to his friend Reddicliffe who had been arrested and questioned in court and who was now cleared).

Mr Wilson: I suggest that the sole motive for you giving information to the police was because you were the ringleader and you were hoping to save your own skin.

Waugh: That is not so.

[The cross questioning was then taken up by Mr Fenwick]

Mr Fenwick: Was any inducement made to you to make this statement.

Waugh: I was sent for.

Mr Fenwick: Your sense of duty had been operating before you were sent for?

Waugh: I did not want to give the fellows away.

Mr Fenwck: They said you were suspected?

Waugh: They did not say that.

Mr Fenwick: Is it your story that you change your suit every day?

Waugh: Every afternoon.

Mr Fenwick: And the change of your suit had nothing to do with the report that one of the wrongdoers could be known by his clothes?

Witness: It was said but I do change my clothes every day.

Mr Fenwick: Will you tell the jury when you changed your suit that day?

Waugh: Yes, I changed my clothes 20 minutes after I got in the house. I always put on an old suit in the morning and change it every afternoon.

Mr Fenwick: You do not change your suit at dinner?

Mr Fenwick: Although you have said that you were 300 yards away from the scene you found it necessary to change your suit. Did you think you might be identified.

Waugh: Yes I did not want to be mixed up with it all.

Mr Fenwick: Does Baker live a few doors from you?

Waugh: Yes.

Mr Fenwick: Is he a man of quite solitary habits?

Waugh: Yes.

Mr Fenwick: Had you any conversation with him the next day.

Waugh: No I had not.

Mr Fenwick: Did Baker say 'It is in the paper we will all get it.'

Waugh: No.

Mr Fenwick: Did you not reply to Baker, 'If they fetch me they'll fetch the lot?'

Waugh: No. That never took place.

[Mr Lowenthal for the prosecution then took up the questioning.]

Mr Lowenthal: Do you want to give evidence against these men?

Waugh: Yes I do now.

Mr Lowenthal: When you were sent for by the police did you make up your mind that you would not give these men away and you made a false statement that you did not know these men?

Waugh: Yes.

Mr Lowenthal: Did you know Reddicliffe had nothing to do with it?

Waugh: Yes.

Mr Lowenthal: Was it the first time you were before magistrates that you said that you would give names?

Waugh: Yes.

Mr Lowenthal: You said to the magistrates that nobody had asked you to give names?

Waugh: Yes I did.

Mr Lowenthal: You said that if you had known the names you would have given them?

Waugh: Yes.

Mr Lowenthal: You also said that having been at the fence you changed your clothes because you did not want to be brought into it?

Waugh: Yes, I have said that before the magistrates.

Mr Lowenthal: Have you come to tell my Lord and the jury the truth before God?

Waugh: I have.

Robert Taylor, miner of Blue Bell Road, was the next witness who gave evidence of going to the High Line. Waugh and Reddicliffe were with him. Reddicliffe left them and went over a field. He [Taylor] saw the men stooping down and they seemed to be lifting the plate. He recognised six men, Stephenson, Harbottle, Muckle, Ellison, Sanderson, and Roberts. Harbottle had a pinch. Stephenson had a big hammer in his hand. The others had nothing. He had known Sanderson about two years, the other five all his life. Witness was about eight yards from the men; Witness said, 'do the lads know what they are doing?' He stayed there three of four minutes only. There were about 20 men on the line. He hurried away when he got to the farm house and the others ran. He ran because he did not want to have anything to do with it. Ellison said at the corner end that he was going to bring every one in who was there whether they were doing anything or nothing.

Cross examined by Mr Wilson, this witness said that the first indication he had of what had happened was when he heard a crash. He was never standing beside the rail. He never saw the engine. He never had a conversation with Waugh about the crash before he went to make a statement to the sergeant. It would be untrue to say that he had agreed with Waugh as to the story they were going to tell the sergeant that they did not know anyone on the line.

Mr Wilson: Why did you alter your statement?

Taylor: Because we were going to get the blame for something we had not done.

Mr Wilson: Did the police threaten to arrest you?

Taylor: No but the man that was with us Reddicliffe was arrested.

Mr Wilson: And you began to be concerned for your own sake?

Taylor: Yes

Mr Wilson: Did you hear anyone say to Waugh he had better change his clothes?

Taylor: No

[The witness was then questioned by Mr Fenwick.]

Mr Fenwick: Did you decide to give evidence against these men from a sense of duty or fear.

Taylor: Both but mostly fear.

Mr Fenwick: When did you first determine to give evidence against these men?

Taylor: The first day we came here. [The police magistrates court at the Moot Hall June 7]

Mr Fenwick: I suggest that you were also on the line amongst the crowd?

Taylor: No.

Mr Fenwick: Do you suggest that of all the men on the line no one was standing by and doing nothing?

Taylor: There were some that were doing nothing.

Mr Fenwick: There were men who were mere spectators that were doing nothing?

Taylor: Quite sure

Mr Fenwick: You spoke, you say, but not very loud. Were you frightened?

Taylor: No.

Mr Fenwick: Did you go to the police or were you sent for?

Taylor: I was sent for.

George Wardle (25) gave evidence of going to the line with the others. Reddicliffe left them and went northwards. He went to where the men were lifting the rail. He was eight yards away. He saw the men who were now in the dock on the line. He knew all the men. He stayed there about four minutes and went home. He was near the farm when he heard the crash and saw the men running towards West Cramlington. At first he refused to give the names but after Reddicliffe was arrested he offered to give the names.

Cross-examined by Mr Wilson Wardle said there had been a lot of men on the line. He saw some men standing around doing nothing. He had not told the truth the first time because he thought he would be brought into it all. He [later] went to see the sergeant.

Mr. Wilson: It was purely a case of fear?

Wardle: Yes.

Mr. Wilson: I suppose you would have had a conference with Taylor and Waugh?

Wardle: No.

Mr. Wilson: Did Taylor and Waugh not tell you what they had said to the Sergeant?

Wardle: No.

Mr. Wilson: You did not know that Taylor and Waugh were to name the people a second time?

Wardle: No I did not go with Taylor and Waugh to the Sergeant although I did go the same day.

Mr. Wilson: I suggest that you and Waugh and Taylor were taking a leading part in the removal of the rail and you simply told this story to save yourselves.

Wardle: No.

Mr Fenwick: I suggest there was a considerable crowd on the line doing nothing?

Wardle: Yes.

Mr Fenwick: Then how is it that you can't remember a man who was doing nothing.

Wardle: I cannot tell.

When evidence for the defence was called William Stephenson told the court that he had gone from the wagon way but had not been on the track side although he had seen men interfering with the rail. He named those men as, Waugh, Taylor, Wardle and Hill all of whom were the prosecution witnesses. Waugh was knocking out the keys, and was heard to say 'haddaway lads, lets make a good job of it.' They then ran away as the steam engine approached.

Robert Harbottle gave an account of his movements. He was with Muckle and Roberts following a big crowd surging towards the bridge over the track. He had seen Waugh and also Arthur Wilson who was holding a hammer but not using it! Waugh had snatched the hammer from Wilson and broke a bolt with it. Then Waugh had used a pinch bar to knock out a chock, which liberated the rail. Then a large group of men lifted the rail out and then ran as the train approached.

Cross-examined by Mr. Lowenthal, Roberts again stated that Taylor, Ellis, Hill, Waugh and Dodds were amongst those that had lifted the rail out of position.

James Ellison said that he had only followed other men to the line and that he had only climbed the telegraph pole in order to look down the line and not in order to cut the wires. He saw Waugh hammering out the chocks and saw that he was wearing a light suit. He also saw Baker who he claimed was only standing watching the activities.

William Muckle's evidence was that it was untrue that he had been involved with the removal of the rail. He had only looked on as Taylor, Wardle, Dodds and Waugh had done the deed.

Oliver Sanderson also stated that the same men removed the rail and that he had watched from a few yards away.

William Baker's evidence was given with difficulty owing to his deafness but he insisted that his purpose at the track side that day was only in order to collect dandelions for his canaries.

Baker was not a miner and not involved in the coal dispute. His deafness excluded him from much of the social life of the village and he claimed only to know four of the other seven accused men.

If at this stage in the trial the jury was looking at the evidence with any degree of objectivity, they could not have avoided the conclusion that the evidence of both sides was essentially the same. Each set of men accused the other of lifting the rail. Each claimed to be innocent bystanders. To convict any of the eight beyond reasonable doubt rested on the credibility of the prosecution witnesses, all of whom admitted that they initially lied to the police. Three admitted that they later changed their stories in fear of being arrested for the crime themselves. They all collectively named the same men although it was generally agreed by both prosecution and defence that many more were involved.

Was it credible that they did not collude in making their statements? Was it credible that the police had not threatened them?

All these questions must have been weighing heavily on the minds of the prosecution when they decided to use the shorthand notes of Richard Bell, the newspaper reporter taken when the nine arrested miners first appeared in the magistrates court on June 7.

The council for the defence strongly objected to this on the grounds that 'the jury may put undue weight to remarks made by men when not legally represented.'

The decision of the Judge, Sir Robert Alderson Wright, was reported by the *Daily Chronicle* on August 2, 1926.

His lordship decided that the evidence should be given and observed that the jury could be trusted not to construe anything into an admission which was not an admission.

The concept of an admission which was not an admission may have tested the finest law brains in the country, never mind a jury of Newcastle businessmen.

However, this allowed Mr Lowenthal to read out some of the questions put to Waugh by the accused at the first hearing. There is no doubt that this sealed the fate of the eight.

Mr Archibald Wilson, in summing up for the defence of Stephenson, Roberts, Harbottle Wilson and Ellison, said that their was no doubt about the facts of the case. He would agree that those responsible had not realised the outcome of their act and it was difficult to understand mob psychology. He urged the jury to consider how ghastly it would be if these men were convicted for merely looking on.

Mr Fenwick said that there was no reliable evidence against Muckle, Sanderson and Baker regarding the displacement of the rail. Men must, he suggested, have been drawn to the scene out of idle curiosity and it was vital that the jury should show no bias and the circumstances of each man should be carefully considered separately.

This point was reiterated by Justice Wright in his summing up:

Someone or other did commit this serious crime but that did not mean necessarily that any or all of the prisoners were guilty of the offence. The jury will have to consider the case against the eight prisoners separately.

A great deal has been made of the fact that if these men are guilty, they are not guilty alone, but there are others concerned. That is a matter you are to put out of your minds because each man has to answer for his own acts. It is not an answer to say 'true I am guilty, but someone else is guilty also.'

The Judge continued saying that the defence argument was that all the eight accused were innocent and that three or more of the witnesses were guilty. 'That might,' he said. 'Have some bearing on the weight you are prepared to give to their evidence.'

> The jury will have to consider the questions put by Baker, Ellison and Wilson to the witnesses at the police court and determine whether they constituted admissions or confessions.

The jury retired at 3.55 pm while the eight accused and their families waited anxiously. Glances and gestures of support went to and fro from the public gallery to the dock. The Jury returned after just 30 minutes.

One by one the foreman of the jury read out the names of the accused declaring each man guilty on both charges. After each man was found guilty an audible gasp of astonishment reverberated throughout the courtroom, but worse was to come. Sanderson, Muckle and Baker were sentenced to serve four years each penal servitude. Stephenson and Ellison to six years penal servitude and finally Harbottle, Wilson and Roberts eight years penal servitude.

The judge added that eight years was as lenient as he could warrant, bearing in mind that they may have been under the influence of others not brought to justice.

The shock of the harsh sentences provoked hysteria amongst the miners' families: women shrieked, cried out in anguish, some fainted, but the judge continued.

> The crime of which the jury, after a very careful and painful hearing, have found you guilty is one of the most serious crimes that can be imagined short of actual murder. If the express, the Flying Scotsman, had been going at a greater pace, in all probability, several fatalities, serious maiming, disabilities and disablements would have occurred. It is only with good fortune that there was no loss of human life.

How young men like you, apparently well behaved and respectable, could have conceived and put into execution so nefarious a scheme has been entirely beyond my comprehension. The evidence however is conclusive. When you have each served your sentences you will still be comparatively young men and will have the world before you. I can only hope that when you have purged your offence by serving your punishment you will lead useful and happy lives.

Court officials were soon attending to the stricken women in the public gallery and a scrum of journalists engulfed the witnesses, fighting for photographs and statements.

When the news of the sentences reached the huge crowd outside the court a menacing buzz of anger pervaded the square. Mounted police were ready and quickly dispersed the crowd to avoid a riot.

The arbitrary harshness of the sentences fuelled the growing resentment in the pit villages of the Northern Coalfield. There was a distinct sense that justice had not been done.

There were many unanswered questions.

If the jury had taken the Judge's direction to consider each man separately then how could they have only taken 30 minutes to reach their verdict?

In his summing up the judge had alluded to the possibility that the evidence of the prosecution witnesses was unreliable and asked them to consider the questions the three men put to the prosecution while not legally represented. If these statements could be construed as admissions of guilt they could only have been admissions of three out of eight of the accused.

We have no report of what Baker said in the police court, but we know that he consistently argued that he was there picking seeds for his canaries. He was not a miner and his deafness isolated him from the community. Surely his case was worthy of more than a few minutes consideration.

For the convicted miners of Cramlington prison was not going to be easy. The majority of the men had never ventured far from their County of Northumberland. They were first taken to Durham prison were they had previously been held on remand. Durham was not too far for family visits and Bill Muckle's girlfriend Dora came to see him as often as she was allowed. However, this was to change and early in August 1926 all the Cramlington miners were moved south to Maidstone prison.

They were moved in two stages, stopping the first night at Leeds Prison, where they learned that there were nearly 100 men in the prison serving sentences for strike-related offences. Next morning they set off for Pentonville prison. They were handcuffed and chained together so that if one wanted to go to the toilet all had to go. As they waited with their guards at Leeds Station for the train to London, they caught sight of the Merry Hampton. They could see it clearly in the sidings, a stark reminder of that fateful day.

Maidstone prison provided little joy for the Cramlington men, now over three hundred miles from their loved ones. Only the food was an improvement on Durham, where they had been half starved.

They were imprisoned in small cells and were separated from each other. They were horrified that they were alongside rapists, thieves and murderers, some serving sentences shorter than they had received. This could have only reinforced their belief that they were pawns in a game of political revenge.

One of their fellow prisoners was Horatio Bottomley, a twice-elected Member of Parliament who had been sentenced for fraud. This man spent a lot of time in the prison hospital where he had special privileges. What outraged the Cramlington men was that Bottomley had the audacity to call the miners, 'silly boys' for getting involved with the derailment.

Muckle was given work as a cleaner in the printer's shop. Sanderson was put to work in the bakehouse, and Baker spent his time in the prison laundry. They were all encouraged to improve their reading, writing and arithmetical skills.

Muckle's was to recall his time in Maidstone 55 years later:

Prison life was prison life in our days. Not a smoke even. Walking out you had to be five yards apart and no talking. You were locked up at 5.15 pm for the night with three books a week to read....

When we went inside they still had arrows on the convict's clothes but as they got washed and wore away they never came back. We had nothing like they have now (as I've heard). We had no wireless or television. Sometime a concert party would come on a Sunday for two hours to fill in the time for us a little bit. We might see a daily paper once a month if lucky! We used to go to church on Sunday morning to hear the chaplain read the football scores out to us.

We were half starved at Durham but when we arrived at Maidstone we got as much bread as we wanted, it being a first offenders prison. On Sunday for dinner you would get a piece of corned beef about the size of the middle of your hand and three spuds some with their coats on with no gravy and a cup of cocoa — that was your whack. You did some funny things inside to get a smoke. If you were caught with tobacco you would lose three months remission with seven days bread and water. I am glad to say it never happened to me.

As I was saying we got bully beef on Sunday and I did not like it. I used to sell it to a lad for two inches of tobacco. He was doing life and had done above six years then. He was allowed to earn 2/6 a month and could spend it on tobacco, but could only smoke twice a day and in one special place. Then it was locked away until the next day when you got the tobacco, or snout as we called it. We used to put some thread around it to make it last. Put it alongside our gum and it stopped there all day. You daren't spit for fear of the warders. I've gone to bed with it in my mouth and no sign of it in the morning but it was well faded then.

None of the men found imprisonment easy but Ellison took his imprisonment particularly hard. Bill Muckle took it upon himself to look for him during the exercise period and they would walk together. Prisoners were not allowed to talk to each other but occasionally a guard would turn a blind eye and allow a few words to be exchanged.

The Cramlington men enjoyed a measure of support from their fellow prisoners and even some prison officers who thought their sentences had been too severe. This made their time in prison a little more bearable. The lock-out was now in its fourth month. Four months without pay, each day harder than the one before, but the daily struggle to survive without means had to continue. The shopowners did their best to help keep them from starving by allowing them some credit. Some shopkeepers baked daily batches of bread and pies filled with whatever was available.

One shopkeeper, Richard Brierley, an ex-miner himself, whose son Peter was also at the Wrighson Pit, kept the general store at High Pit with his wife Mary Ann. They had worked hard to supply food to the striking families and allowed as much credit as they were able. Now after four months their ability to sustain such generosity was under sever strain.

Miners however were not strangers to the hardships of strikes and had over the years developed a kind of welfare state within the communities. The Co-op store was the centre of activity in most villages and the Co-operative Societies were in the main run by miners. With support from the Co-op bank the local stores offered credit to miners which was usually underwritten by the local Lodge of the Northumberland Miners' Association. This meant that the local union was responsible for calling in the debt, making the Co-op privileged creditors, which often worked to the detriment of the local shopkeepers who had given credit.

Feeding centres were run by the union and food was begged from the surrounding countryside. Miners' gardens provided fresh vegetables, pigs and poultry.

Rabbits and fish and the odd pheasant could be obtained, not always strictly according to the law. Miners and Mechanics Institutes' Methodist Chapels and Pubs all became venues for concerts organised by local musicians to help the cause.

Even in the best of times child mortality in the northern pit villages was high. Childhood diseases and malnutrition claimed many young lives

Richard and Mary Ann Brierley outside their shop at High Pit Cramlington

Miners at play, 1926 strike

Miners children scavenging for coal 1926 strike

Children collecting food 1926 strike

Street corner meeting, miners strike 1926

and despite the best efforts of the community these premature deaths continued during the strike.

While many came to the aid of the mining communities there were others who were actively hostile, blaming the miners for bringing hardship on themselves.

At the start of the strike one mine-owner's agent reported to his boss that the miners had no idea of the merits of the dispute.

They draw 'lying in' pay on Friday which they use for their own amusement, gambling and beer, leaving the feeding of their families to be done by those better off. They have a fair chance of holding out for quite a while because so much money is going into the villages in the form of state pensions and benefits, ex-soldiers' pensions, compensation, Guardians relief and health insurance.

He also complained that men were stealing coal from their pits in order to sell for gain.

One advantage the miners had was the weather. Throughout the summer of 1926 the sun shone with an uncharacteristic consistency and the Northern Coalfield remained in the main solidly on strike. In the Midlands it was another story. By the end of October 58,000 of the 97,000 miners had returned work and as the strike weakened the mine-owners, sensing outright victory, became more opposed to negotiating with the MFGB. On November 12 the MFGB gave each area the power to negotiate a

LORD MAYOR'S CHAMBER,
TOWN HALL,
NEWCASTLE UPON TYNE.

BC.

3rd November. 1926.

My dear Sir,

Referring to correspondence which has passed between Sir Nicholas Grattan Doyle and yourself, I can quite appreciate that, in view of the extraordinarily heavy demands upon your time, you do not see your way to grant me the interview which I asked Sir Nicholas to endeavour to obtain for me. I also appreciate very much your kind offer to receive any representations in writing from me, and, in taking advantage of this privilege, I shall be as brief as possible.

My views are that, having regard to the ages of the culprits involved in the Cramlington Railway outrage, the young men had their passions inflamed by older men who ought to have known much better, and that, whilst they were guilty of a very serious offence, these young men did not realise the terrible nature of their crime.

I venture to express the opinion that justice would be met and that it would have a great moral effect on the Mining community, which would not be deprecated by the community as a whole, if the sentences were reduced by fifty or even seventy-five per cent.

I have some knowledge of the Mining fraternity, being, as a matter of fact, the Son of a Collier myself. I have moved amongst these people practically all my life, and I think I may claim to have an unusual knowledge of their good points as well as of their defects.

I should like to state that, in endeavouring to approach you in this matter, I am not acting under the influence of any individual whatever, or of any party. I am solely actuated by a strong desire to see whether a little mercy shown in this direction would have a useful effect not only upon those who are now undergoing punishment, but also upon those whom they have left behind and upon the whole of the Mining industry.

I feel sure that you will give this matter your consideration when time permits.

Believe me,
Yours faithfully,

Anthony Oates

Lord Mayor.

Sir Wm. Joynson Hicks,
Home Secretary,
Home Office,
Whitehall,
LONDON, S.W.

return to work on an area basis. By the end of November all areas were back at work working longer hours for less money.

From the first day the men were sentenced a campaign was launched throughout the labour movement to get them released.

The MFGB constantly lobbied Parliament protesting at the severity of the sentences, their complaints falling on deaf Conservative ears.

Even the Lord Mayor of Newcastle was moved to write to Sir William Joynson Hicks the Home Secretary on November 3, 1926.

My views are that having regard to the ages of the culprits involved in the Cramlington Rail Outrage, the young men had their passions inflamed by older men who ought to have known better and that while these men have been found guilty of a serious offence they did not realise the terrible nature of their crime.

I venture to express my opinion that justice would be met and that it would have a great moral effect on the mining community which would not be depreciated by the community as a whole if sentences were reduced by 50% or even 75%.

I have some knowledge of the mining fraternity being as a matter of fact the son of a collier myself. I have moved amongst these people practically all my life, and I think I can claim unusual knowledge of their good points as well as their defects.

I should like to state that in endeavouring to approach you in this matter I am not acting under he influence of any individual or party. I am solely actuated by a strong desire to see whether a little mercy shown in this direction would have a useful effect, not only on those who are now undergoing punishment, but those who have been left behind and upon the whole of the mining industry.

The most consistent campaign was undertaken by a Communist organisation called the International Class War Prisoners Aid (ICWPA). A remarkable woman called Sarah Lovell from this organisation visited all the families of the jailed men to give what aid she could. She raised sufficient money for travel and accommodation so the families could visit Maidstone prison every six months for the 30 minutes they were allowed to share with their loved ones.

She campaigned tirelessly for the release of the miners and with their wives and mothers held a rally in Trafalgar Square where banners proclaimed, 'Free the Cramlington Miners.'

The most left-wing paper of the day was the *Sunday Worker,* which proclaimed on its banner head *The Sunday Worker — The Sunday Paper of the Labour Movement.* This paper became the mouthpiece of the campaign. In its enthusiasm to have the men released it published an article on August 22, 1926 proclaiming that the Cramlington men had been framed by 'provocative agents.'

> Was the wreck of the Flying Scotsman a frame-up against active strike leaders?

The crash had been caused, they argued, 'entirely by the bad driving of the scabs' and that the rail had been removed after the accident to implicate the miners.

Sarah Lovell

FRAME-UP ?

RAIL TAMPERED WITH AFTER SMASH ?

Eight Miners Jailed, But Belief in Innocence Widespread

PROVOCATIVE AGENTS

Were They Responsible for Boss Plot to Involve Strikers ?

Was the wreck of the "Flying Scotsman" a frame-up against active strike leaders?

The SUNDAY WORKER is able to-day to give for the first time the inside story of the wreck of the "Flying Scotsman" at Cramlington, near Newcastle, on May 10, in the last days of the General Strike.

It will be remembered that eight young miners were sentenced to periods varying from four to eight years on a charge of wrecking the train, but the feeling in the district is that those who bore witness against them knew more about the affair than the imprisoned men.

The men were accused of tampering with the rails, but photographs reproduced on this page show that the metals were tampered with *after* the accident.

The whole affair looks like a frame-up of the worst description. Durham Labour leaders are taking up the case of these men, and call for a united Labour campaign on their behalf.

CAMPAIGN FOR RELEASE

Well-known Miners' Leaders Appeal to the Labour Movement

Sunday Worker August 22, 1926

While no one in Cramlington could have possibly believed this account of the derailment, such was the atmosphere of mistrust that many trade union branches referred to this theory in resolutions supporting the Cramlington men which were sent to the TUC and Labour Party.

The issue was even raised at the annual conference of the TUC in 1929. F Rowland, a delegate from the House and Ship Painters Union, objected to the 1928 TUC annual report that condemned the ICWPA as a 'front for Moscow.'

In moving a reference back of the offending paragraph Rowland declared that there were many members of the General Council and delegates in the hall who associated themselves with the ICWPA.

And I offer no apologies for being associated with any working-class body that has the interests of the struggling masses as its object....

As far as the miners at Cramlington are concerned, they were put in prison on very doubtful evidence. (Cries of no) I say they were put in prison on very doubtful evidence. The photographs show that it was inclined to be a 'frame-up.'

The Home Office was inundated with resolutions and letters calling for the release of the imprisoned men, perhaps the most poignant was a plea from Robert Harbottle's mother. She wrote in March 1928:

Dear Sir,

Can you do something towards helping my son Robert Harbottle who is serving 8 years penal servitude for the Cramlington Railway Smash during the general strike of 1926.

It is breaking our hearts to think that he and other seven have to serve terms of 4,6 and 8 years for the wrong-doing of 40 and the wringleaders [sic] going about scot free.

I have 6 sons and 1 daughter and I have never had a days trouble with one of them until this has happened and I am 63 years old and my husband is 66 years of age and I think it will kill us if there is nothing done towards helping him out.

We can prove that man broke the bolt to start the moving of the line and I think is hard seeing him going about and my son shut away for eight years.

My son was a good boy at home and he went to church regularly. He was the one who kept the home together.

I don't know how he got mixed up in this as he never went about with any of the men who were up the line. I have just received a first class Ambulance Certificate from him so you see he is still working, as he did at home.

We are very much against the Communists here making a fuss about

25 Lane Road,
West Cramlington.
Northumberland.
March 26th

Dear Sir,

Can you do anything towards helping my son Robert Harbottle who is serving 8 years penal servitude for the Cramlington Railway Smash during the General Strike of 1926.

It is breaking our hearts to think that he and other seven have to serve terms of 4, 6 and 8 years for the wrong-doing of 40 and the wrong-leaders going about scot free.

I have 6 sons and 1 daughter and I have never had a days trouble with one of them until this has happened and I am 63 years and my husband is 66 years of age and I think it will kill us if there is nothing done towards helping him out.

We can prove that 1 man broke the bolt to start the removing of the

First page of Mrs Harbottles letter

it as we don't believe in Communism.

It would not have been so hard to bear if they had all got the same time or if they could all be released together. My son is the youngest of the eight who are prisoners at Maidstone. I hope you will be able to do something for him.

Yours Truly,

Mrs Harbottle

The campaign was effective and on August 24, 1928, 'as an act of pure clemency,' the Tory Home Secretary recommended a reduction of sentences for all eight of the Cramlington miners. After consulting the trial Judge and in view of the prisoners' good character before the derailment, Muckle, Baker and Sanderson would be released from Maidstone prison on September 1, 1929. Ellison and Stephenson would have their six year sentence reduced to four years and Wilson, Roberts and Harbottle from eight years to five.

The *Sunday Worker,* while welcoming the reductions as 'a triumph for the agitation carried out by the ICWPA,' asserted that clemency was not enough and reiterated its claim that the miners had been framed.

On Saturday September 1, 1928 after serving two years and three months of their sentence, Muckle, Baker and Sanderson stepped out of Maidstone prison to be greeted by a small group of supporters, one carrying a red flag. In each of their lapels was a red rose given to them by their fellow prisoners. One supporter shouted,

The Union Jack got you in here but the Red Flag got you out.

Baker and Sanderson were greeted by their wives and Muckle by his mother. Muckle's girlfriend Dora had long since stopped visiting. They were taken for a proper fried breakfast before making the journey to London, where a welcoming rally was to be held the following day at Poplar Town Hall.

They were to stay overnight at the address of an ICWPA supporter. This man was not in at their time of calling, so they all went to the pictures,

ICWPA rally for the release of the Cramlington miners in Trafalgar Square

a luxury that they had been deprived of for some time.

On the Monday morning Muckle recalled that they bought the newspapers before travelling to Kings Cross Station, where they had to make a mad dash to catch their train to Newcastle. The train was packed and they stood in the corridors for most of their journey, but they were free for the first time for over two years to stretch their legs where and when they wanted. They could chat together and reflect on the time they had spent in prison. They arrived at Newcastle central station at 6.56 pm to a rapturous reception.

Covertly watching their arrival was a plain clothes detective who filed the following report to the deputy chief constable:

I beg to state that three of the Cramlington train wreckers who were quite recently released from prison after receiving a remission of their sentence arrived at the Central Station at 6.56 on the 3rd inst'.

To witness the arrival of these men there would be assembled at the station about 3,000 people.

On the main square at the entrance to No 6 platform a Guard of Honour was formed of about eight young members of the LLX wearing khaki uniforms, red ties and khaki caps with red bands, there were also members of the ICWPA present. The train wreckers on alighting from the train posed for their photographs which appeared in the Newcastle Daily Chronicle and the North Mail on the 4th inst.

On reaching the main square from No 8 platform they received rousing cheers and the reception they got was that of heroes.

There were people on the edge of the crowd in the station who enquired what was on and when they were told they exclaimed that the affair was a disgrace to civilisation.

Below: Photograph taken shorty after the prisoners release from Maidstone jail. l to r: Sanderson and wife, Muckle and mothe, Baker and wife.

Released men and their families arrive at Newcastle Central Station

Members of the Communist Party were prominent and as they marched out of the station the 'Red Flag' was sung.

They marched through the various streets to the Haymarket where a meeting of the Communist Party was held, the three Cramlington men being on the platform for a short time before leaving for Cramlington.

The speakers on the platform were Comrades Will Lawther, Thirbeck and Cohen. Each of these speakers referred to the release of the three men and they stated that it was a "great victory" for the Communist Party as the Capitalist Class was the party who sent the men to prison.

Cohen stated that Joynson Hicks [Tory Home Secretary] had released the three Cramlington miners thinking that it would keep the CP quiet, but he never made such a mistake in his life as they — the Communist Party — would never rest until the walls of the prison were opened and the other five Cramlington men were released, also that they would agitate until all the "class war" prisoners were released and Capitalism smashed, it was also suggested that the releasing of the men was merely device for vote catching by the Conservative Party—the Capitalist Class.

Much was said by Thirlbeck of Sunderland to maintain the doctrine of the ICWPA and he asked the workers to unite to the Communist Party as being the only party out for the welfare of the "working classes"

He held up Soviet Russia as an example. He stated that he had been to that country and the working class in that country were all content with the wages and conditions under which they worked.

The speaker also referred to an incident which happened in Sunderland only a day or two ago, where , he said, women members of the party were assaulted [by the police] and their underclothing torn from them, one he stated received a black eye.

He held the police up to ridicule and said that they were only puppets of the Capitalist Class.

Members of the party got out collecting boxes and commenced to take a collection but were at once stopped from doing so by the police. The meeting concluded by singing the " Red Flag" and the crowd dispersed.

When the three released men left the meeting to go to Cramlington they could not get on the bus due to the large number of people now returning to Cramlington so they retired to the Clayton Arms and enjoyed a few gills of beer.

They eventually made their way first to Dudley where they were met by another huge crowd and welcoming reception and more speeches were delivered.

When they finally reached Cramlington a huge crowed packed the Co-op hall to welcome them home. The Women's Guild presented them with 30 shillings each and when Muckle thanked them from the platform the effect of the beer and rich food overcame him and he had to rush to the back of the hall and into the toilets to be sick.

On September 15 in the same Hall another packed meeting the miners were presented with gold medals by Alex Gossip, Vice Chairman of the *Sunday Worker.*

In the weeks to follow the released men were all feted as heroes, attending many meetings to report their experiences and to campaign for the release of their comrades still imprisoned in Maidstone Jail. Even Sergeant Graham was seen to push drinking money into the hands of the released men.

After three weeks Muckle got casual work at Dudley pit, where he loaded ten-and-a-half-ton trucks for 2s 10p (30p) a truck. He later recalled that after the first day he was so stiff he couldn't sit down for two days.

Life had been hard for miners before the 1926 strike and worse after. In 1929 it was to get much worse.

At first there was a glimmer of hope when the Labour Party won the General Election on May 30, 1929. However they failed to achieve and overall majority and relied on the votes of the Liberal Party to govern.

All demands by the ICWPA for the new government to declare a general amnesty for all class war prisoners fell on deaf ears despite having the support of some left-wing MPs. However, by July 1929 Ellison and Stephenson were due for release on licence. The three years they spent in Maidstone jail and the year's remission they had earned completed their reduced sentences. Consequently they were informed they would be released on the morning of Friday July 12, and their wives travelled down to London on the Wednesday of that week to greet them at the gates of the prison.

The ICWPA organised a welcoming rally for Sunday July 14 in Trafalgar Square and an all-night vigil at the jail on Thursday night until the expected release on Friday. When the Home Office got wind of these arrangements they sent word to the prison governor to bring the release date forward to the Thursday morning and to immediately put the miners on a train for Newcastle. When Ellison and Stephenson protested that their wives were in London and there was no one at home they were told that these were the orders of the Home Office and had to be obeyed.

On reaching Newcastle on Thursday evening the two miners immediately boarded the next train bound for London and were reunited with their wives. When they returned to Newcastle on the Monday they were received by a large crowd and treated to the same reception as had been enjoyed by Muckle, Baker and Sanderson.

Ellen Wilkinson, the MP for Jarrow, was so incensed by the manner in which the men had been released that she wrote an angry letter to JR Clynes, the Home Secretary, describing his actions as 'administrative cruelty' and predicting 'wild indignation in the area.'

The remaining three Cramlington miners were just three years and three months into their sentence when the world was turned upside down by the Wall Street Crash. The stock market in the USA had reached a pinnacle of value in the first week of September. Between October 24 and 29 there was a wave of panic selling and the market crashed. Shares in industry and banking became almost worthless and almost over night 100,000 businesses in America closed down, throwing millions out of work. The effects of this catastrophe reverberated around the world and the Northern Coalfield was hit badly. The misery of unemployment and short-time working was to last for a decade.

For the Communists in the ICWPA the Wall Street Crash and the mass unemployment it created must have looked very much like the collapse of the Capitalist System they had predicted. The Communist Party, which had only been founded in 1922, was still a relatively small party but it was making progress. In 1926 it had doubled its numbers from 5,000 to over 10,000 members, mostly recruited from the mining villages. Its ability to go to the heart of the Cramlington community with practical aid and win the support of many prominent trade unionists and left MPs must have weighed heavily on the minds of the Labour Government.

The Communist Party was also at work in the heart of MacDonald's constituency, where the 3,800 miners at Dawdon colliery, Seaham Harbour in County Durham were locked out on March 2, 1929 because they refused to accept a further reduction in their conditions. Another Communist front organisation known as Workers International Relief (WIR) led by James Ancrum, a Gateshead Communist councillor, set up a kitchen in the village and organised financial support that became crucial to the miners ability to hold out for five months. Harry Pollitt, the leader of the Communist Party, had addressed a 2,000 strong meeting in Dawdon on May Day and stood against MacDonald in the General Election.

It is impossible to say what role the threat of the growing influence of the Communist Party played in the release of the remaining prisoners, but Clynes, the new Labour Home Secretary ordered their release just before Christmas 1929.

At about this time the Home Secretary visited the prison, a duty he took on about twice a year, and after taking tea with the Governor there was a tradition to discuss the early release of any deserving prisoners. The Governor in turn would ask the Chief Prison Officer who would nominate a few men. These would all be paraded before the Governor in his study and the Home Secretary would give a lecture on 'going straight' and they would be released within 24 hours.

The final three miners, Wilson, Roberts and Harbottle were the 'chosen ones.' They were cautioned not to get in touch with the press or the ICWPA and not to rally in London.

The early release was a complete surprise and a wonderful Christmas present for their families. They arrived home just two days before Christmas. They had served three and a half years of the eight years sentence they received at the Moot Hall. The ICWPA and the campaigners had at last succeeded in gaining the release of all eight miners and that Christmas was call for great celebration within the families and the villagers of Cramlington.

24. xii. 29.

My dear Clynes:

Very many thanks for your letter of the 23rd December concerning Arthur Wilson and the rest of the Cramlington miners.

I am very glad indeed to hear that they have now been released and would like to congratulate you on making the decision which will bring happiness into the homes of these three men.

Yours very truly,

George Lansbury

Letter from George Lansbury, Labour Commissioner of Works, to Home Secretary Clynes on the release of the last three prisoners

Chapter 4
No Regrets

From left to right: Harbottle, Muckle, Wilson and Roberts.   photo taken by Newcastle Evening Chronicle 1965

James Ellison, who had suffered most in Maidstone jail, tragically died shortly after being released from prison.

Wilson found work at the nearby Dudley colliery while Muckle, Roberts, Sanderson, Harbottle and Stephenson returned eventually to work at Wrightson pit alongside the very men who had turned king's evidence and had betrayed them.

Tom Roberts worked on the coal face alongside Waugh, the chief witness upon whose evidence he had been sentenced to eight years imprisonment. He even played football for the same team — Roberts in goal, Waugh full-back. In an interview in 1965 Roberts told the Evening Chronicle, 'We never said anything about it. What was the point in saying anything?'

Tom Roberts married in 1930 and in the five consecutive years that followed his wife gave birth to a child each year. All five children died shortly after birth and then in 1939 Tom's wife died. He remarried in 1941.

On May 1969, the London to Aberdeen overnight express crashed just south of Morpeth killing six passengers. In the early hours of the morning a local doctor rushed to the scene to tend the injured. This doctor was Snowdon Blaiklock, who 43 years earlier as a young medical student worked as a volunteer guard on the Flying Scotsmen. The publicity surrounding this accident awoke memories of the Cramlington incident and inspired a BBC 2's Yesterdays Witness programme to interview Roberts, Wilson, Muckle and Harbottle, the four surviving miners.

In this half-hour programme Harbottle explained how he had come to terms with his imprisonment,

> I said let the past go. I paid for it and it was finished with. It was for me anyway. It wasn't with William Muckle and Arthur Wilson but for me it was over with. Best left alone.

Muckle was less forgiving,

> They did the job the same as we did. We got time and they should have done time too. They did a rotten dirty trick. Mind they were looked down on. Folk wouldn't speak to them.

> I went to the club one night and one of the witnesses came up to me and said, 'Will you have a drink off me Bill?' I said, 'I don't want a drink off you. If I had any poison in me pocket I would put it in your beer now,' and he started to cry. Never seen him no more.

Wilson was the least forgiving, as Roberts was to testify,

> When a witness would die — big celebrations! Arthur would send word up — Come down! — Whisky! Arthur provided the whisky. He's got a bottle in now for the last one. Queer lad Arthur.

Bill Muckle with wife Jenny, 1969

Wilson explained that he ran a campaign of hatred against the witnesses, spoiling their gardens. With a wry smile on his face he recalled,

> One night I came home and I saw one [of the witnesses] tight — drunk. When he came past I teemed a bucket of water over him. He never said nothing.

> One morning I went to the club and got the whiskies in. They said, 'what's up.' I said, 'we're celebrating. We're celebrating a death. Waughy's deed!'

Wilson, Muckle and Roberts were unrepentant. Given the same circumstance they would do the same thing again.

Muckle said,

> We had to do something similar to what we did do to show people

what we were getting. I used to say we were slaves. We were on starvation wages.

Muckle was later to write:

I never did regret what I did and I never will. We were fighting for our daily bread. When you come to think of the wages of the Government and the Royal Family and their understrappers, you can go mad. What with Lords and Ladies and their like taking the best of the land. I worked 52 years in the pit to my sorrow. In our day you had very little chance to do anything else. In 1926 there might have been a revolution. It was a very near thing. The rich are doing their best to keep the working class down. They always have done. As I have said, there is no call for these lords and ladies. We should do the same as Russia did and clear them out.

All confessed to being happy and having had a good life. Roberts was particularly resilient despite the tragedy of his first marriage.

The Governor of Durham Jail said to me that he would take the smile off my face but they never did, it's still there. No one will take the smile off my face 'cos I take hardships as they come. I've been gruelled into it.

The four miners were not able to see the programme as they hadn't televisions that could receive BBC 2. One person who did see it however was Sarah Lovell, who had been so important to the men and their families so many years before. Her husband Bob had recently died and she had wanted to write his biography. She wrote to Muckle and Roberts for information of their involvement with the ICWPA and eventually, with their friendship renewed, she came to Cramlington to stay with the Roberts family. They never forgot her or how her organisation had helped them all in their time of need.

In 1981 Bill Muckle wrote a short memoir called *No Regrets,* which was published by The People's Publications. In it he gave an insight into the hardships of pit life before and after the 1926 lock-out, and he made an astonishing confession.

Fifty five years ago and nobody knows to this day that I and three others broke into the railwaymen's cabin and stole the gear in the morning (before the meeting) for the job in the afternoon. This never came out in the trial and we never told this to the papers or the television.

Muckle explained how he had told the lads after the meeting to come to the line in the afternoon and ' we will have a rail up.'

When they saw that the train was the Flying Scotsman they were horrified and one man was on the bridge waving a handkerchief to warn the engine driver.

Muckle continued,

We were miners content with what we had, only if they had let us alone; but they came for a 40% cut in our wages and that put our backs up. The only thing I was sorry about was that the train we tipped was The Flying Scotsman with 281 people aboard. I say now that we were thankful there was nobody killed (just one man had his foot hurt), but when you come to think again it was a General Strike and there were blacklegs running the trains.

Bill had married his sweetheart Jenny in 1932 . She died on January 20, 1981 before the book was published. Bill's final words are a tribute to Jenny:

Finally, I would like to say farewell to my best pal Jenny. She was a good person and came from Backworth. We had a good life together....
...May whoever is up there bless her, she was one of the best.

Perhaps the most telling comment was made by Roberts, who when asked by a BBC 2 reporter in 1969 why he described his life as one of happiness, he replied 'Because we had a community.'

Bill Muckle was to see the final battle for those mining communities. He died in the winter of 1984 in the middle of the year-long miners' strike.

Afterword

Shortly after the end of the miners' strike, 1926, Richard Brierley the ex-miner who kept the general store at High Pit faced ruin. For six months no one had money to spend in his shop and much of the credit he had given his customers was not repaid. Miners now on reduced earnings found it impossible to feed their families and repay their debt. Trade never recovered as families, too embarrassed to face Richard and his wife Mary Ann, deserted the shop.

When the business failed Richard, Mary Ann and their two youngest sons journeyed south to London where Richard acquired a job on the railways. He took with him a wad of newspapers reporting the wrecking of the Flying Scotsman and the subsequent trial.

Many years later he showed his granddaughter the now yellowing bundle of cuttings which inspired this book.

Sources

May 1926 — The General Strike, Chistopher Farman

No Regrets, William Muckle

General Strike in the North East, Anthony Mason

Behind the scenes of the Great Strike, Hamilton Fyfe

The Miners — Years of Struggle, R Page Arnot

Yesterdays Witness, BBC 2 video

Public Records Office Kew

Newcastle Chronicle and Journal —Central Library, Newcastle

Northumberland County Records

Cramlington Library

Marx Memorial Library, London